THE POETIC DRAMA
OF PAUL CLAUDEL

THE
POETIC DRAMA OF
PAUL CLAUDEL

by

Joseph Chiari

GORDIAN PRESS
NEW YORK
1969

First Published 1954

Reprinted 1969 by Gordian Press, Inc.
by arrangement with Harvil Press, Ltd.

Library of Congress Catalog Card Number 71-90365

CONTENTS

		PAGE
	Introduction	I
Chapter I.	Drama and Poetry	23
II.	Beginning: *Tête d'or*	46
III.	Early Plays: *La Ville, Le Repos du Septième Jour, L'Échange*	54
IV.	*Partage de Midi*	66
V.	*La jeune fille Violaine, L'Annonce faite à Marie* ..	74
VI.	*Le Soulier de Satin*	87
VII.	*L'Otage, Le Pain dur, Le Père Humilié*	115
VIII.	Theology and Love in Claudel	129
IX.	Claudel as a Poet	139
X.	Claudel's Art Poétique..	145
XI.	Concluding Remarks	166
	Note I	173
	Note II	175
	Bibliography	179

INTRODUCTION

THE subject of this study is Claudel's poetic drama; in order that one may see clearly its worth, one needs to relate it closely to its background, which is our age. Now, just as, in Nature, every aspect of matter—whether it is oil, coal or gold—is found only in certain definite geological backgrounds, in the same way, in human life one does not find an Alexander Pope sitting side by side at the Mermaid Tavern with Shakespeare or Marlowe, or a Voltaire joining the many outings of La Fontaine, Racine, and Molière. That does not mean that the picture of any given age can ever present the kind of homo-geneity suggested by literary historians, intent on submitting life to analytical processes and on viewing it in patterns of integrated movements and reactions to these movements. Whether in life or in history, there is at work a process of development or of growth which ensures that certain things, events, or manifestations of the spirit can take place only at certain moments and not at others. All things are immutably related, and happen, or become part of the phenomenal world and history, in their due time. The ages of great drama were ages in which not only a form of expression had been evolved, but in which there was also a kind of expectancy for the very things that were to come. Such was the age of Shakespeare and that of Racine. Everything seemed to have been prepared for these men, who were the crowning peaks of ages in which reality was like a broad-based pyramid tapering off towards the invisible heights of supra-reality.

Great art has flourished only in 'religious' ages. 'Re-ligious', in this context, is meant to convey something which transcends man and offers him a depth of experience which ranges from the human to the metaphysical plane. Although it is agreed that religion and art are two different aspects of the human experience, they have many affinities, many similari-ties, and they are the only two human experiences which

[1]

involve the whole being; they are the only two forms of true knowledge. Greek drama was essentially religious, and therefore expressed the very life of the people who were witnessing it. The age of Shakespeare was also 'religious', despite the fact that we cannot ascribe Shakespeare to any Church. He sprang from a religious age; like Pascal, he feared the infinite spaces and the silences where his soul might be lost, and he prayed God for lasting peace. Marlowe's atheism presupposes theism, and Marlowe is perhaps nearer the angels than many who were disturbed by his vocal atheism. Dr. Faustus is much given to certain aspects of life which Renaissance man prized highly—beauty, search for knowledge, and love of power and pleasure—but he is no unbeliever, and in the end, brow-beaten by the Devil and forbidden to repent, he cries:

O, I'll leap up to my God!—who pulls me down?—
See, see, where Christ's blood streams in the firmament!

—while the chorus answers:

Cut is the branch that might have grown full straight.

We feel that his good angel could have saved him, or perhaps that, like Goethe's Faust, his imperfections are part of the eternal order of things, within God's will.

The Elizabethan age and the age of Racine were, to a large extent, dramatic ages, ages of movement and action, when tragedy could be lived on the stage. Ours is, on the contrary, a tragic age,[1] an age of suffering and widespread awareness of man's desperate plight; one cannot be surprised that the human beings who have endured the concentration camps or the bombing of Berlin, London, or Hiroshima find it difficult to accept tragedy and pathos on the stage, and prefer the realistic or escapist atmosphere of the cinema and the ballet, or plays and films whose dramatic tension and continuous excitement are the only means of keeping their already overstrained sensations at a high pitch.

In our age we witness, side by side, the crudest materialism in everyday life and the most childish sentimentalism in the various forms of entertainment; and, strange as it may seem,

[1] See Note I.

[2]

both materialism and sentimentalism are covered by the more attractive label of realism. The cinema is more 'realistic' than the theatre, yet its realism seems to concentrate on the satisfaction of the crudest animal instincts. The theatre wrongly tries to compete with it by overstressing the visual and realistic aspect of things. The result is that in this competition between visual and auditory senses all possibilities of poetry are lost; one cannot enjoy at the same time the Sixth Symphony of Beethoven and the beauty of a Constable or the poetry of *The Tempest*. Each one of these artistic creations is complete in itself, and requires our undivided attention. In this age of the star, who has become an element necessary to attract a wide public to any play, and of the equally 'starred and star-minded' producer, who must in each production spring a surprise on his public, the cost of the production of any play is such that it can be accepted only if it is popular—and popularity, in this case, means, in England, conformity with the pattern of a London West-End comedy, or in France a *comédie de boulevard*.

The ballet has perhaps been responsible for a greater interest in formal beauty, but it has also been the source of certain analogies between ballet and poetic drama which do not stand the test of examination. It has been said that just as the choreographer leaves a certain amount of initiative to the ballet-dancer who creates poetry by movement, in the same way the poet should leave a certain amount of initiative to the actors by providing them with certain choreographic guidances. People talk freely of a dancer being a poet. He may be a poet if he writes poetry, but he certainly cannot write it with the arabesques of his arms and legs; what he can do and what he does is to create in spectators who have sensitiveness and imagination a 'poetic' state, and if any one of those spectators is a poet, he will transmute the experience undergone into poetry. Poetry is not a state, but a crystallization of that state into an object or a fixed form. A painter can be a poet, a composer can be a poet; a dancer may have the most poetical soul alive, but cannot be a poet through dance,[1]

[1] Poetry is analogical to dance, as it is analogical to music, but it is neither.

because poetry is oneness; it implies a synthesis, an imaginative unity which can be born only from one single mind, and not from a collaboration of people, such as playwright, producer, stage designer, actor, and public. Poetry is in the word, or is not, and though scenery, star-acting, and incidental music can create a poetical impression, they cannot create poetry. If there is poetry in a play, the word rightly spoken by the actor should suffice.

The analogy with music, the conviction that a play lives only when it is acted, as music lives only when it is played, is not exact, for a symphony, or any musical composition, has first and foremost been felt and brought together as one living thing by the composer, and is not the result of a co-operation. Although conductors and musicians may mar it, or squeeze the last ounce of life out of its notes, it exists as a living thing, irrespective of conductors and musicians. The musicians are only the instruments who make apprehensible to the senses of the uninitiated something which exists already, in the same way as the actor should only be the servant of the author's words. There are plays which do not bear reading and only live on the stage through the skill of the actors, but that is because they are inferior plays and certainly not poetry. But the greatest plays—those of Shakespeare or those of Racine and others—can give as much enjoyment, if not more, when read as when acted. Those plays were written by men who knew what they were doing, and they knew what poetry was; they knew that it did not require the help of operatic scenery. As Hamlet says, ' the play is the thing ', and the actors of those days trusted the words which they could aptly deliver anywhere, in a courtyard or in the most austere setting; they did not require Rubens or Teniers to paint the scenery, or Purcell or Lulli to add music.

William Archer complained that there were no tears in Shakespeare—even Juliet does not weep when Romeo leaves her. Shakespeare knew better. Poetry is an objectification of feelings and thoughts, a way of presenting feelings and thoughts through actions, events, objects, symbols, or myths. Art is not a display of tears or other forms of emotion, but a means of bringing emotion to other people's hearts and minds, and except in cases of mass hysteria, this is obtained by words and not by sobs and exclamations.[1] Paolo and Francesca together read a book describing a love which is also theirs, and they fall into each other's arms, but we may be sure that nothing would have happened if, instead of reading about the love of Lancelot and Guinevere, they had merely read that Lancelot and Guinevere, overwhelmed with desire, kissed each other. The kind of development which Archer seems to have anticipated is the visual art—the cinema; but we must remember that love-poetry is poetry and not merely love-making, as is so often the case in films or in bad plays which make use of mimetism, one of the strongest *instincts* of men. That point, together with his continuous insistence on ' reality ' and ' realism ' in art and on the need to dissociate lyricism and drama, show clearly the kind of tragedy which Archer had in mind. Tragedy is not reality, at least in the everyday meaning of the word; it is not life, it deals only with the affective key-points or knots of life, with the projections of the essences of life. The poet transmutes feelings and emotions into imaginative creations which, to be on a high level, must stand by their own strength, just as a child must live his own life and not be a shadow or a projection of his parents. It is only in creations which have reached this state of objectification, finality, and purity that we have greatness and lasting beauty. Goethe, for instance, in spite of his greatness, does not succeed in severing the pre-natal cord between himself and his great poem *Faust*. Faust cannot live without Goethe, in the same way as Phèdre lives without Racine, or Othello and Hamlet without Shakespeare. *Faust* is perhaps rather an epic than a drama, and it presents the producers who wish to stage it with well-nigh insuperable difficulties. In fact, Goethe seems to have failed to grasp the truth which Milton so readily understood, that the supernatural, with angels and daemons, is a subject which is more fit for epic than for drama.

---

[1] Nothing illustrates better the difference between emotions—the raw material of poetry—and their transmutation into poetry, than a brief comparison between the sentimentality of Lamartine and the crispness of his contemporary, Keats. Everything comes from the poet, but experience only becomes valid once it has been intensified, enriched with memories, and fused into poetic creations which have an imaginative life of their own.

Besides this, the tragic stature of Faust is considerably diminished by the fact that the riddle of the conflict between good and evil is not left unsolved as in Shakespearean, Greek, or Racinian tragedies, but gives a Spinozan solution: that it was part of the greater good.

There are mysteries which are beyond man's grasp, and the broken flight, if the aim was lofty, is a sign of supreme greatness and not of weakness; the heart of Hamlet, the Gioconda's smile, are unfathomable mysteries which fascinate men confronted by something which is life, and yet is beyond life. To think that the poet can sit down and behave like the master of a complex puppet-show, who knows exactly what gestures, what movements his figures are going to perform, is to ignore the very essence of poetry. One may write *Candida* or *Arms and the Man* in that way—they are brilliant demonstrations of dialectical power—but one cannot write *Hamlet, Macbeth,* or *King Lear* in this way, for they are attempts to probe through poetry into mysteries that are part of the very texture of the human mind and can be glimpsed at only in rare moments of illumination, and then not without mortal danger. T. S. Eliot's lines from *The Dry Salvages* convey, better than anything else I know, the experience of illumination and complete union between the thing and the seer in a timeless moment:

> For most of us, there is only the unattended
> Moment, the moment in and out of time . . .

Poetry is language endowed with revelatory power, therefore used as a metaphysical instrument capable of unveiling the essential truths which exist in all things created—a stone, a heart, or a city alley. Poetry cannot therefore be a matter of subject—beautiful or ugly, ' poetic ' or realistic—for poetry can be found in all things if the poet has the necessary vision and the imagination to transport himself into the heart of whatever it is he contemplates; it is a matter of source, of inner, essential life, and not of appearances, dazzling veils floating on air. True poetry is the utterance, the revelation of some of the mystery of Nature, of life itself; it is a voice whose echoes will live as long as time, it is the vision of things

[6]

as they will be, as they are eternally. Poetry is the eruption
through man, part of Nature, of the forces which are life
seen *sub specie æternitatis*. The men who have felt such eruptions
are few, and the moments in which they felt them very rare:

> There was a time when meadow, grove and stream,
> The earth, and every common sight,
>   To me did seem
> Apparelled in celestial light,
> The glory and the freshness of a dream,

said one of the greatest poets, and yet he spent perhaps most
of his life asking himself:

> Whither is fled the visionary gleam?
> Where is it now, the glory and the dream?

Poetry had fled, the flower at his feet could speak no more;
he could hear no more the true voice of things. Yet he ful-
filled his purpose because, for a moment, through him, as
through the other few who lived before and after him, life
had cast up reflections and visions which form the very pattern
of human existence, in the same way as in Christ—God made
man—we have had a revelation of the very source and end of
life. The intensity, the frequency, and the duration of the
visions vary according to the poet; Wordsworth had spent
barely a third of his life when he wrote:

> The things which I have seen I now can see no more.

On the other hand, Shakespeare and Racine, a few years
before their deaths, could still soar to empyrean heights and
give us their final vision of the world in creations which, like
The Tempest and *Athalie*, reveal the poet's insight into the true
essence of things, and the metaphysical force of language. In
both cases we are beyond the human, in realms where life has
regained its true perspective in a pattern which transcends it.
Joad's words: *Je crains Dieu, cher Abner, et n'ai point d'autre
crainte*, are echoed by Prospero's conviction that all human
agitations and actions fade into nothing:

> The solemn temples, the great globe itself,
> Yea, all which it inherit, shall dissolve,
> And, like this insubstantial pageant faded,
> Leave not a rack behind . . .

—after which he begs leave to go and rest his ' beating mind ' : indeed, such supra-human visions set the mind beating, and the soul trembling.

The true poet knows that poetry is everywhere in life, for the mystery is part of life; he can gaze with child-like eyes upon things and situations which seem to the ordinary man as common and worn-out as the cobbles of the road, and he can descry in them part of the mystery which trembles in Œdipus' fate or sets Prospero's heart beating. He knows unerringly that whatever his powers as a poet, he must begin from the beginning, from the source, the centre of things, and not try to delude himself and others by juggling with shapes and empty forms which, however mighty, can only derive their life and brilliance from the substance which men of great vision once infused into them. It seems that it is the very nature, the essence of the true poet to be unable to accept as poetry the outward form of an experience which is not his own. He may have had once only in his life the vision which, henceforth, remembering Wordsworth's moving words, he will long to recover, but if he has once known what poetry is, if he has experienced that grace, he will never be able to compromise; he will bemoan his loss, he will suffer, he will keep hoping that other visitations may take place, but he will not try to delude himself or others. If he is a poet, even if he has had only glimpses of the glory and the dream, he will know that there are various degrees of poetry, that one poet may write *Alexander's Feast* or *Don Juan* and *The Vision of Judgment*, while another may write *The Ancient Mariner* or the *Ode to a Nightingale*; he will know that in each case the poetry must rise from the thing itself, from the theme experienced, but he will never try to delude himself and others with the suggestion that if he put Sophocles' or Shakespeare's mask on his head he might speak with their voices, or that certain names, certain places, themes, and situations can be enough to make poetry. True, hearts can beat in the same way under a Greek chlamys, a brocade dress, tweeds, or a cotton frock, and it is in these beats that poetry lies; but it is the poetry which must be revealed, or it will die, killed by those who, perhaps not knowing what it is, spread the idea that it can live only in the mist of history or on the shores of the ancient world.

The problem here raised is vital; it is not the problem of the contrast between realistic and historical, epic, mythical, or idealized subjects, neither is it the problem of the contrast between flamboyant rhetoric or highly ' imaged ' poetry and poetry which seems to be very near to prose; it is the problem which concerns the difference between true poetry and all kinds of devices and themes which have associations with poetry and which have certain apparent poetic qualities, but which are not poetry. Why, says the man in the street, should he hear only of mythological or legendary characters such as Orestes, Pelléas, Mélisande, or some moonstruck queen of Ruritania, when he has felt in himself the whip of the Eumenides or the torments of an impossible love? Why can he not watch on the stage the aches and pains of men and women born in Manchester or in Lyons, instead of being forever lost in the dust of the Grecian roads or in some ghostly palace of forgotten ages? This background confirms him in his view that poetry is some rare hothouse plant which can only be seen or described with all the care and preparation required to observe an eclipse or a comet; and that can only lead him to feel that it is all very well for Antigone or King Mark to express love and hate in poetry, but that twentieth-century lovers can never speak to each other in such exalted and ' unreal ' tones, for if they did so, they would be merely ' acting '. It is with the heart that the poet must start, and not with the golden east or with the machinery of the stage. If men must rise above the earth, if saintly souls must journey to Heaven, it can only be by the power of the heart and words which can lift us, and not with rope and flying pigeons, as in some of Cocteau's plays. If Eliot has achieved the most remarkable success of our time in the theatre, it is because, with the integrity which characterizes him, he refused to put his trust in devices or to attempt to give us the shadow for the substance. As a poet—one of the greatest poets of our time— he knows the poetic value of myths, and he has the true gift of the poet, the power to go to the source, so that the poetry is born from inner tensions and is not a matter of external forms. He has closely studied Greek, Elizabethan, and French drama, and his characters undertake Euripidean journeys to rescue souls. His plays have strange subterranean links with the myths which arose with the dawn of our civilization; they show subtle kinship with the works of minds which discovered, in the depth of the heart, certain age-old upsurges which rock it to destruction, whether the heart beats on the shores of the Pyrrheus or on the banks of the Thames. They show the kind of truth which lives on the stage or off the stage, the truth which enabled Racine to give Phèdre, prisoner of the moon, that unfathomable depth of human passion which, from the Minoan palace where she was born, has lifted her right through the ages on to heights beyond the reach of men and time's alterations. This is indeed myth brought to life, taken as it was, and offered to men and women who knew of the life of Athens or Rome, and although it is permeated with Christianity, it has retained the sense of the *numinous*. What makes Phèdre as alive to-day as she was at the Court of Louis XIV, is the poetic revelation of a truth which shakes the husk of names and ages, and reaches the perennial texture of Being. To do that, to see so far, a man must have in himself some strange means to link up with the sources of Being. Racine and other great poets had such means of revealing what is, and yet lies beyond men's gaze.

In my opinion Eliot, more than any other poet of our time, has this power to reach to the sources. The result is that his laying bare of the human consciousness can give his poetry or his dramatic creations the force which makes us feel what we truly are. His success throws into relief the weaknesses of poetic drama in France and elsewhere. In England, for instance, the theatre of his contemporary, Christopher Fry, is the best example of the lack of the very quality which Eliot possesses—imaginative insight. Fry's glittering poetry has caught the public mind, but how long will it hold it? Even more, will it be capable of progress? I hope so, though I have doubts. Fry is undoubtedly a poet, a man who has the gift of words, of striking phrases, and of brilliant authentic images and conceits, a man of wit, who can intermingle the love of men with the revolutions of the stars; yet in spite of *The*

Firstborn, his best play, he has not shown a deep sense of
drama, because he lacks that imaginative sensitiveness which
sees life in everything. His words, however pleasing, have no
deep roots in human hearts; they are firework displays,
fascinating to watch, yet fading into utter darkness; they are
an end in themselves, and not, as in Eliot, a beginning—the
light on the miner's helmet as he walks down into the bowels
of the earth. In spite of his great verbal felicity and freshness
of vision, Fry's plots wear thin, for the characters are shallow,
and one wonders at the cause of a verbal inebriation which
makes one think of birds trying to out-sing one another for the
mere pleasure of doing so. There is also another problem
connected with these plays. Owing to their lack of characterization and dramatic plot, and their reliance on ' mood ' or
atmosphere, they can be brought to life only by first-rate
actors who can add substance to the gossamer-like, delicate
verbal magic. Still, we should be grateful for what Mr. Fry
has already achieved.

The situation of poetic drama in France to-day is not as
good as it is in England. In 1924, when Copeau retired from
the stage, the impact of German stagecraft and theatre was
already beginning to make itself felt, and it soon acquired a
detrimental influence. The conception of Gordon Craig and
of Copeau—that the producer was the supreme authority in
charge of the play—existed also in Germany, where it had a
very peculiar evolution. The producer became the all-in-all
of the play. Whereas, in France, Copeau had concentrated all
his efforts on the words, in Germany they were the least
important aspect of the producer's cares. What mattered
was success. The play did not require to be acted, it was
interpreted. The producer could do what he liked with it:
he could shorten it, lengthen it, patch it up, transform it into
something unrecognizable. Germany's theatre after the First
World War seemed to have had the single preoccupation
of producing a dreamland where people could for a few hours
escape from the drab life which confronted them. The theatre
became the enchanted palace of some Kubla Khan. The
people who moved about in it were clad in an unearthly way;
tramps and kings wore the same luxurious brocades tailored

by the greatest houses of fashion. The Germans are, on the whole, escapists, hence the formidable danger which still confronts us; they very quickly forget the past, their surroundings and their cruel deeds, and are painfully surprised when the rest of the world does not do the same. They forget everything except their dreams, whose gossamer holds together the pagan and the Christian worlds. The fatality of Cain seems to weigh on them, and they stumble forward amidst the rubble of broken worlds, never more proud than when they die in a Wagnerian apotheosis of the loosened elements falling all round like the last bars of a supernal symphony. They dream perhaps of a magnificent fifth act to the drama of the life of mankind, in which this old planet explodes into fragments engulfing in its destruction the German people hurling a last shout of defiance at nothingness. They dream too much, and as they are at the extreme point of subjectivity, they take these dreams for reality and live their tragedies. Goethe knew this weakness all too well when he went to Italy in search of the calm detachment of its classical tradition, and when he married Faustus to Helena; he knew that unless he controlled his emotions, his emotions would overwhelm him, as they overwhelmed Nietzsche and Hölderlin, and he felt that both the man and the artist must control their material, whether it be in life or in art.

The French theatre, in spite of the wars (or because of them), has been influenced by the German theatre, to a much greater extent than the English. The French are on the whole a happy-go-lucky people, who do not live their tragedies and do not confuse art and real life; nevertheless, the combined influence of Russian ballet and German staging has gained ground in France and has greatly offset the good teaching of Copeau. This love of machinery and of impressive scenery is all the more difficult to understand in a people well endowed with visual imagination and in love with words. The influence of the ballet, coupled perhaps with a return to mime, is obviously at work on an actor like J.-L. Barrault, who performs with his whole body as well as with words. The trend inaugurated by Copeau has been superseded by various schools of thought, all tending towards the belief, best expounded by

Cocteau, that the poetry of a play is the result of a co-operation between producer, actor, and audience, and exists only during the performance. There is no need to stress again the shallowness of such a view. Jouvet could make Giraudoux show certain attributes of poetry, but no amount of good staging and good acting—and Jouvet could provide both—can transform *Ondine* into a poem, for it is not a poem, although it is packed with inchoate material which, with sufficient transmutation, might become poetry.

The same criterion applies to Cocteau's and to Anouilh's theatre, which cannot be described as poetic drama. Copeau's simplicity of staging has now been replaced by the rich sceneries of Christian Bérard and Gaston Baty, and by the striking productions of Barrault and Jouvet's other successors, who continue to make Paris the outstanding world centre of the theatre. If they do not produce poetic drama, it is not their fault, but the fault of the poets. Jouvet has given new life to Molière and made Giraudoux's great reputation, and Barrault has produced and acted in the two greatest theatrical events which France has known for many years—*Partage de Midi* and *Le Soulier de Satin*.

And here we reach Paul Claudel, one of the most important poet-dramatists of our time. He is definitely a major poet, and if one cannot be carried away by M. Madaule's enthusiasm and pronounce his name in the same breath as those of Homer, Virgil, or Dante, one cannot fail to detect traces of the same visions which illuminate the works of those writers. Those visions are possibly too sparse, too insubstantial in Claudel to give his name the aura of supreme greatness; on the other hand, it may be too early to pronounce a judgment which can stand the test of time, and one might be inclined to think that one ought to wait for the generations to come to do this. Yet, looking round in our times, and looking back across the field of the world's literature, it is not difficult to see that Claudel already occupies a high position. He is in some ways enormous. He looks like an uncouth primal being, who can epitomize the various manifestations and aspects of Nature. Certainly he can rise to awe-inspiring grandeur but also flounder into appalling platitudes, lack of taste and critical judgment.

His name unfailingly recalls that of Victor Hugo, with whom he shares an exuberance of language and a visionary power unsurpassed in French literature, and even a casual acquaintance with his work makes one realize that he has upon him the unmistakable marks of genius.

Genius is a wide word whose range encompasses Dante and Donne; it is a word which implies certain definite heights but no absolute universal level. Besides this, it suggests a natural facility and also a kind of one-sidedness which require to be combined with other elements in order to produce highly integrated creations. I have no doubt that Victor Hugo was a greater genius than Baudelaire, yet I feel that Baudelaire was perhaps the greater poet of the two, and that Racine, who combines the excellence of both, was a greater poet than either of them. We may have to revise our approach to the meaning of the word ' genius ' and come closer to the ideal of serenity and empyrean mastery advocated by Goethe. We may have to endeavour to realize that genius consists perhaps just as much in the refusal to let come to life anything but the elements necessary to the whole, as in the ability to bring to life, in one whole, the most divine harmonies and the most cacophonous sounds. That selective aspect of genius cannot be confused with talents; it is consciousness at its highest point, it is the infra-godlike power which orchestrated the harmonies of Shakespeare's great plays, it is the power which, on a different level, produced *The Rime of the Ancient Mariner, La Jeune Parque,* and *Four Quartets,* but it is not the one which produced *Alexander's Feast, The Scholar Gypsy, Elegy in a Country Churchyard,* or some of Ronsard's odes. Here indeed we have manifestations of extraordinary talent, but nothing more, by which I do not mean to imply that the authors of these poems have no claims to the title of geniuses—far from it; indeed, two of them—the first and the last—are major poets and amongst the great geniuses of the world. Yet I doubt if there is any one of their poems which could be called great in the same way as one could call great *Four Quartets* or *An Ode on Intimations of Immortality.* I am aware of the imprecision of my argument, and I am even more aware that if pressed too far, it could easily lead to untenable positions. Yet I cannot but stress the point that the gifts which enable a poet to have an all-embracing imaginative vision of the world and to express it in words endowed with the power to sweep the whole range of man's memory and to reach beyond it, are of a different order from those which enable him to give formal beauty to a thought, an event, or an experience which has neither depth nor universality. Claudel is the most extraordinary genius of our time, yet I have the feeling that Valéry, Eliot, or Yeats may be greater poets than he is, and that Eliot's poetic drama may also be greater than his; for if the graphs of these poets' creations do not shoot up like sharp needles to Claudelian heights, they never sink to the depths to which those of Claudel sometimes fall. In short, however important it may be, the excellence of a work of art cannot be altogether determined by a few dazzling flights into space. The flights must be sustained, with ups and downs, of course, but the graph must not be that of a very undulating temperature. Such achievements require a special tempo of breathing, but they also require a steady pulse. My feeling is that Claudel's pulse is not steady enough, and that is why I cannot place him on the topmost pinnacle where some of his enthusiastic admirers have set him; yet I share to the full their conviction that he is a major poet, and one of the greatest of our time.

A prolific writer, who has explored many fields of literary expression, Claudel is first and foremost a poet who has written what is described as lyrical poetry and, above all, poetic dramas. He has at times succeeded, and he has possibly produced great drama, but even when he has failed, he has produced often enough outstanding poetry. It is obvious that William Archer's distinction between poetry and drama is impossible to uphold in the field which we are examining. One may or may not succeed in discriminating between the subtle shades of meaning involved, yet we shall easily see that in poetic drama a failure in poetry entails a failure in drama, for the drama is contained in the poetry. One can hardly dissent from T. S. Eliot's view that Shakespeare was a greater dramatist than Ibsen, because he was a greater poet. On the other hand, it is possible, often enough, for a poet to fail to write good poetic drama, and yet to write some very good poetry; what happens is that, even if the poet has failed in his main task—which was to give to the dramatic poem a wholeness which characterizes organic life—he may have succeeded in writing passages which in themselves are good poetry, even although they are not quite in character nor congruent to the oneness of the dramatic poem.

In prose drama the words, essentially informative and not creative, preserve their logical, analytical meaning, and their apprehension remains, on the whole, at the conscious level. This kind of apprehension is not inferior to the poetic apprehension, but it is incomplete, because it does not involve the whole being, which comprises the subconscious; therefore we have no oneness of experience either in the creative mind or in the spectator's or reader's. It is true that in prose drama we do not necessarily have the same division between subject and object that we have in comedy; but if our consciousness is not temporarily and as far as possible spellbound (and that can be done only by true poetry), we remain always on the alert, ready to dissociate subject and object, and our pleasure, though sustained, does not have the intensity and the richness of an experience which can, for a moment, abolish time. In the end, the great dramatist is the great poet. That does not mean that a great poet is necessarily a great dramatist; Dante was a great poet, yet, although he wrote dramatic poetry, he is not a dramatist. Another important fact to be borne in mind is that if we allow our views of poetic drama to be bound by certain conventions which have been recognized as the basis of that genre, Sophocles or Racine could be put forward as being greater dramatists than Shakespeare. That may be so, and one might even argue that had Shakespeare worked within certain conventions, he might have risen higher; yet the important fact is that the work of a great writer is the expression of his genius related to, and transcending, his age. Sophocles and Racine lived in ages when certain dramatic conventions were accepted as natural, and therefore beyond discussion, while Shakespeare lived in an age of growth and fluidity of thought and artistic expression. And there remains the incontrovertible fact that a poet may produce creations which may not be as flawless as those of others, but whose beauty, though at some points rugged or even stained with defects, will nevertheless shine further and brighter because of the poetic imagination which gave it birth. This is perhaps the case with Shakespeare, whose plays, though they may not have the structural perfection of those of Corneille or of Racine, are on the whole greater dramas, because they are greater poetry. But there is yet another aspect to this problem which requires examination; for, having suggested that Shakespeare, because he was a greater poet is also a greater poet dramatist than Racine or Corneille, one could find oneself accepting the inference that Shelley, because he was a greater poet, was also a greater dramatist than W. B. Yeats. That inference is not verified by history. W. B. Yeats is recognized as a better dramatist than either Shelley or Swinburne. This is because he has a clearer and more concrete visual imagination, and also a greater sense of drama than either of them, though as a poet he may not have had Swinburne's mastery of words or Shelley's visionary power.

Whether one deals with lyrical or with dramatic poetry,[1] one cannot avoid thinking that where Claudel fails in either instance, this failure springs from the same source. He has a Shelleyan impatience with the material which he uses, and he is inclined to become over-concerned with the beliefs—intellectual or affective—which he wishes to convey. His imagination, like Shelley's, can operate on a cosmic scale, but he has neither the precision of the other great romantics who, like Coleridge and Wordsworth, could rise to the ideal world through reality and the senses, nor the apocalyptic vividness of a poet who, like Blake, trusted his inner eye and ear more than his perceptions. Claudel's symbolism is imprecise and woolly, and he constantly shows that kind of arrested poetic process which characterizes Victor Hugo, who so often floats in the limbo world which lies between the abstract concept and the concrete sensuous realization of the creations of the mind. Often enough, Claudel is neither a philosopher nor a poet, but a hybrid conglomeration of both, as Shelley and Victor Hugo so often are. He has not succeeded, as Dante has done, in transmuting a philosophy into poetry, nor has he been able

[1] See Note II.

[17]

to reach philosophy and the mysteries of life, as the greatest have done, through the intuitive tentacles of poetry. Either out of sheer impatience or from imprecision of vision, he often presents us with vast, vague, and sonorous creations which might or might not catch reflections of the human soul, while he hopes that the reader or the listener may supply what is missing and grasp the whole. Yet, in fact, vagueness of expression can only breed vagueness of reception, and the imagination must either be allowed to work freely on its own, or, if it is to be orientated towards definite ends, it can get on the right road only by being supplied with experiences which have the outward precision of sensuous apprehensions. The sounds and visions conveyed must be endowed with the quality of audibility and visibility, and for that they must have been clearly heard or seen by the poet. All too often such is not the case with Claudel or Victor Hugo, who are apt to content themselves with a verbal vagueness which gives only the illusion of the real thing. The result is language for language's sake, and not language used as a means to an end, as the source of the image of the real thing. The words are accepted, or rather chosen, as an end in themselves, just as the visions of things are not those which can rise from their true nature, but those which the poet wants to see in order to reach his goal. In the end we are faced with a deliberate wilfulness towards the words, and towards the worlds which they try to create, and that is something which implies definitely set personalities and no possible attitude of ' negative capability '. This does not annul the extraordinary gifts which these men possess, but it does mean that they have assumed in the course of their lives a set character or a persona which has sometimes dominated, sometimes come to terms with the poet, who has been at times servant, and only rarely the master of that character. Yet, since that character must have developed from forces inherent in the poet, there are also moments of perfect union when character and poet blend harmoniously.

This is not an inquiry into the whole complex range of Claudel's dramatic work—a task which would involve an examination of the origins, the structure, the various versions and characters of the plays, together with certain inevitable problems of ethics and style—it is an attempt to find what could be called poetic drama in the most significant works of Claudel, and what kind of poetic drama it is. The aim of this study is to try to show that an analysis of the dramatic structure of the main plays may enable one to conclude that what counts most in the case of Claudel, as in the case of all poet drama-tists, is neither dramatic structure nor power of characteriza-tion, but the poetic value (that is to say, the imaginative truth and beauty) of the work as a whole. An attempt of this kind cannot fail to involve an appraisal of Claudel's gifts as a poet writing for the theatre, his mastery of words, his control of design, and the revelatory power of the language as the expression of the auditory and visual imagination bringing to life experiences of perennial worth. My contention is that the apprehension of the work of a poet who, like Claudel, has so uncompromisingly sought to follow the bent of his in-genius, would suffer untold damage if the work were judged by the disciplines and rules which Claudel has deliberately and completely ignored. A great innovator in verse, and above all possessed of the most powerful imagination which has been at work in French literature since Victor Hugo, Claudel is a poet whose works must first and foremost be con-sidered as an imaginative synthesis. If we neglect the pre-eminence of the imagination, if we attach too much importance to the psychology of the characters and to the logic of the action, if we isolate those aspects of drama from the poetic pattern which contains both and is more important than they are, we shall be over-emphasizing certain aspects of the plays to the detriment of others, and we shall severely curtail our apprecia-tion of the whole. If, on the contrary, we do what one ought always to do with poet dramatists, if we give pre-eminence of attention to poetic wholeness and think more in terms of symbolism and imaginative truths than in terms of character and logical development of actions and situations, we shall preserve unbroken the subtle imaginative texture of each play and we shall see it as an harmonious whole.

It is true, of course, that Claudel writes in terms of drama, but the dramatic nature of his work cannot be used, when dealing with poetic drama, as the only basis for an interpretation or a critical appreciation of that work. In the end it is nothing more than a convention used in order to express certain truths which were in the poet. That convention has its importance, and when a poet writes for the stage, one has the right to ask oneself whether or not he has succeeded in producing drama; yet when dealing with poetic drama, what finally counts is not drama, but the dramatic poem. The examination of the dramatic structure of a poetic drama can be used, and should be used, as a means to throw light on certain aspects of the work, yet in order to have an all-embracing and complex grasp of that work one must try to reach the imaginative core which determines its nature and gives it its reality. I am aware of the fact that in adopting this standpoint I implicitly insist upon the primacy of æsthetic value in art, a value which transcends all other aspects, such as sources, intentions, characters, and ethics, and in its wider significance contains them all. Yet what surely counts in a work of art is its imaginative truth, a truth which is the highest form of beauty, and a truth in which ethics are in the end a matter of æsthetic achievement. One must be wary of confusing the morality of human life and the morality of dramatic characters; if we did this, we might apply purely social criteria of morality to characters and to actions which should be judged only in relation to the wholeness of the work of art, and therefore in relation to life on the transcendental plane of art.

The mind must needs have an object for its inquiry, and when it comes to analysis it can deal with only one thing at a time. Yet poetry, or any form of art, remains at its best an expression of the whole being, something which contains mind and is also more complex, more transcendental than any human mind. An intellectual reconstruction may or may not add to our enjoyment and appreciation of a work of art, yet it seems to me that if one wants to have a complete appreciation of its range, complexity, and living beauty, one has to try to grasp it, as much as possible, imaginatively, as a whole whose fragile, tenuous life enchants our eyes, a whole which, if pulled to pieces, would leave us with only coloured dust on our fingers, as when we attempt to lay hands on the multicoloured wings of a butterfly. An examination of the pattern, structure, and components of the various colours is not forbidden, nor would it preclude our enjoyment of the beauty of the whole, but it would singularly diminish the range and quality of our æsthetic emotions if we focused our attention on any one of these points in isolation from the others.

To begin with, Claudel is not a psychologist; he may be unable to descry the intricate workings of the human heart, or he may not be interested in those workings except inasmuch as they correspond to certain aspects of his imaginative vision of the cosmos, which, so far as results are concerned, comes to the same thing. He is not concerned, like Shaw or Sartre, with the propagation of certain philosophical and moral beliefs and ideas in terms of human psychology and human behaviour; he is a poet, and as such he is concerned with expressing and conveying to men the truth which lies at the centre of his whole being, in terms of symbols, metaphors, analogies, and images. The truth which Claudel feels is God's truth; the structure of life and of the cosmos which he descries is not the one seen by the bodily eye, but the one seen by the inner eye of the imagination, and the way in which he attempts to express his vision is by means which make of his characters, actions, and situations the second terms of analogies, or the words or objects standing for vast images, metaphors, and forces which lie beyond the seeing eye and are part of a pattern in which eternity touches time only at certain points and through the medium of the creative mind. Therefore, if we wish to recapture glimmers of the vision which filled the poet's eye, we must not attempt to give those terms, characters, or situations an intrinsic, self-contained, logical meaning, but consider them as the apprehensible signs of vast constructions which might be glimpsed at, but which can be apprehended, as far as that is possible, only in a referential way. If we examine the plays from the vantage point of poetic oneness, we may even feel that certain flat passages, halts in the progress of the action, and flaws in the growth of characters could be considered, even in their negative values, as parts of the symphonic structure of the plays (I have in mind modern symphonies, and not those of Mozart or Beethoven). They may be necessary to throw into relief certain other aspects

[21]

which perhaps can fit into the whole only when set into that kind of dull or negative context. I do not wish to imply that all weaknesses of style, construction, or characterization are willed or could be explained away in that fashion; I merely mean to suggest that those weaknesses would lose a great deal of their sharpness of relief if viewed as the possibly necessary dull colours of landscape which may be closely scrutinized in its details, but which should be finally contemplated from a distance and as a fully integrated whole.

In order to attempt to understand and to appraise the work of Claudel or any other important poet-dramatist, one must view their work not only in the climate of their time but also against the background of the historical development of poetic drama and in the light of the ideals and achievements of other poet-dramatists of the past. In order to have a picture of Claudel's poetic drama, one needs to have present in the mind the main points of the evolution of poetic drama since its inception, together with some idea of the fundamental problems that the writing of poetic drama involves. One cannot hope to produce within the context of this study an outline of poetic drama which could be comprehensive or even informative enough for the layman; volumes have been written on the subject, and I shall confine myself to trying to point out certain salient features which may throw some light on the road I am endeavouring to follow, and on the conclusions which can be reached. Then, once we have present in the mind a picture of the evolution of poetic drama, and once we have narrowed the field of possible disagreement about the meaning of such words as tragedy, pathos, drama, etc., a brief examination of the structure of each play should enable us to see what kind of poetic drama Claudel's is, and from what vantage point it should be surveyed in order to perceive it as something *sui generis* and in order to come to a possible assessment of its worth.

DRAMA AND POETRY

TRAGEDY can take place only on the metaphysical plane, on the plane of the great conflict between man and God or man and the gods. But why, one may ask, if life is God-created, do men have these impulses and divergencies against God's Will? Possibly because each thing, in order to exist, implies its opposite, just as being implies non-being, yet the opposites are resolved into the apparent oneness of being. Tragedy is religious without being the servant of religion, and moral without any explicit morality. As for psychology preceding metaphysics, as Gide says in his essay in *L'évolution du théâtre*, this seems to be putting the cart before the horse, the contingent before the essence; what one calls moral feeling is a religious feeling inherent in man and which transcends Paganism and historical Christianity. It is the vague awareness, varying in intensity according to the individual, of being or not being in accord with God's Will, source of life. The Greek myths—those of Œdipus, Phædra, Antigone, etc.—must have sprung from human consciousness, and found expression in personages of flesh and blood because they are part of the human consciousness. The problems involved are problems of the human consciousness.

Poets, with their intuitive knowledge of the human consciousness, have embodied those conflicts which take place in the human soul into realities apprehensible to the senses; the fact that they can, in that way, be experienced by readers or listeners should, according to Aristotle, help to resolve those conflicts, those 'guilty' passions in the human soul which by its essence should tend to remain within God's Will. Bearing that point in mind, a dramatic action is bound to be a crisis, or it is nothing, for since it is the concretization of some of the most fundamental conflicts of the human consciousness, its embodiment in tragedy must retain the aspect of concentrated crisis. Since the characters of the drama stand for certain destructive forces in human consciousness, and are opposed to life as being God's Will, the solution of such a crisis can be found only in death; and the main aim of tragedy is, above all, to produce in the heart of the *dramatis personæ*, in the human consciousness, that absolute knowledge which sees in death the only way to return to God's Will, the way which makes of death a rebirth. Death may not imply the immediate return into God's Will; Phædra knows that even in death her guilt and suffering will continue, but she knows that they will continue as part of the process of purification, and she knows intuitively that she will return to God, and that is why she accepts death.

The plight of a man crushed by supra-human odds is tragic and pathetic; his struggle against those odds—if struggle there is—is dramatic and implies uncertainty and suspense. Tragedy always contains pathos, but not necessarily drama, that is to say suspense and doubts as to the *dénouement*; far from it; the great tragedies of Aeschylus, Sophocles, and even of Euripides, are not ' dramatic ', but mostly centred on the pathos of terror and undeserved suffering. Pathos can be derived from various sources; in the Greek tragedies the most important ones were the following:

(1) far too great a disproportion between certain acts willed or innocently performed, and their consequences;

(2) the ruthless punishment of certain passions which are beyond the control of those who endure them, or of errors whose consequences are much heavier than the errors themselves;

(3) the punishment for acts which, however horrifying, were performed in a complete state of ignorance of their import, and willed by superior unavoidable forces;

(4) the suffering of innocent victims at the hands of characters who, in a moment of violence, forget their most natural relationships.

The evolution of Greek tragedy began with Euripides, in whose plays the characters sometimes use their power of speech to justify themselves or their ends, and not to sing their

sorrows. In Euripides, the chorus ceases to be always a part
of the action and is often used as a lyrical interlude in which
the action is halted; here we have the first steps which led
to the separation between lyricism and drama. Psychology
and psychopathology, which were to play such an important
part in seventeenth-century drama, make their appearance
with Euripides. Senecan tragedy marks a great step forward
towards drama, since the element of struggle becomes predominant, and is strengthened by the fact that the hero—a
true Stoic—endeavours to assume the complete mastery of his
self and of all the various forces and circumstances which are
part of his environment.

With Corneille the idea of the plot, which has evolved from
Latin comedy through tragi-comedy, becomes all-important;
it must be a well-knit pattern in which each scene, with its
complete interplay of feelings, passion, and interests, helps or
holds back the final solution. The pole of interest has shifted
from the passion born from the suffering of the hero, to the
psychological conflict, dramatic tension, and suspense which
lead to the *dénouement*. Since the progress of the action has
become the mainspring of the drama, the action, in order to
be easily followed, must be simple, and the problem must be
clearly stated at the beginning in an exposition, which must
contain the seeds of all the developments that are to follow.
The *dénouement* must answer all the questions that have been
raised and leave no character hanging in the air; and above
all, it must flow directly from the premises of the exposition.
No external event, no *deus ex machina* must intervene; the
machine set in motion at the beginning must run smoothly
and with precision to the end in an atmosphere of psychological
verisimilitude.

Corneille is not concerned with pathos, but with psychological
motives; he prefers characters who, instead of being torn by
conflicting forces or crushed by inescapable, merciless blows,
know where they are going and why they are doing certain
things; his characters are generally individuals of extraordinary
will-power based on reason and clear judgment. They know
what to choose, what to do, and once their decisions have been
taken in the light of reason, they carry them out without fear

or pity in a Nietzschean grandeur which seems to rise above everything—death included. Whatever happens, the Corneillean hero controls his destiny; that is why Corneille rejects the theory of the imperfect tragic hero of Aristotle. What he is concerned with is greatness and moral truths, and therefore saints and heroes who are perfect, or villains who are completely evil, dominate his theatre. He is not concerned with purgation of passions but with resemblances to life; he does not want to excite our pity by the sight of man's helplessness and suffering, but rather to animate our admiration and our faith in human nature, by a vision of grandeur and of human freedom. Therefore he requires something nobler than love, something which will never go beyond the dominion of a reason which controls the will. In his theatre there may be passions, but they must always be graded and controlled by reason; Pauline begins by being in love with Sévère—the perfect Roman gentleman—but when Polyeucte, by offering his life and soul to God, rises to a higher plane of human achievement, Pauline naturally gives him all her affection and love, and is ready to follow him to martyrdom and death. Horace's fanatical patriotism leads him to kill his sister, who has rationalized her passions for Curiace to the point of rousing her brother's patriotic anger to the necessary pitch. It is all perhaps rather on the level of concept and rationalization than on that of integrated, yet random life. The results of this kind of philosophy of life are clearly visible in Corneille's last plays, which tend to be more and more mechanical; indeed, he ended by shutting himself into an impossible dilemma. On the one hand, since the hero is a man of will, one could not let him wait four acts to decide what he was going to do in the fifth; will can be defined only in action, the hero's will must therefore be constantly fed so that he may exercise it and maintain it alive; therefore a series of obstacles have to be provided in order to maintain that will in being; consequently one gets a certain mechanicalness and incidents for incidents' sake. On the other hand, if the will becomes fixed in a perfect supra-human clarity of vision, action stops; for, once one has reached that state where the human soul can look, from a kind of empyrean detachment, upon anything unscared, no movement remains worthwhile. Therefore in the end Corneille returned to a conception which saw tragedy as the representation of great souls, not overwhelmed by supra-human forces, but calmly accepting their fate. There is in this type of tragedy a lyricism of expression, which does not arise from suffering, but is rather the result of introspective examinations and an expression of all alternatives, each one calmly rejected. As the hero is never broken by his destiny, which he majestically and freely accepts, there is no pathos; so we have merely a series of subtle analyses of varying length and relevance.

Racine maintained the psychological truth of the characters, the dramatic interest, and, to a certain extent, the plot, but he moved far away from Corneille, towards the world of the Greeks and of poetry. I have no intention of probing into the reasons which may have contributed to the differences between Racine's and Corneille's dramatic creations; sufficient to say that Racine was a different type of poet. He was a much greater poet, and a truer poet than Corneille, whose limited imaginative range prevented him from reaching the depth of mystery which Racine could reach. One of the problems which each writer of genius has to face is that of reconciling as far as possible the bent of his individual genius with the conventions, moods, expectations, and outward artistic forms of his time. There were conventions, moods, expectations, and forms which Racine could not hope, or was not concerned, to change. He felt that he could rise, carrying them all on his wings as unavoidable necessities which would in no way impede his flight. A truly great poet cannot be fettered by anything; he may be compelled to struggle harder with the medium he uses and the situations which face him than he would have had to had he lived in other times, yet from the compressions and efforts of this struggle a great strength may be generated which may propel him higher on to planes of radiant beauty which he might never have reached had it not been for some of the narrow channels he had to force himself through.

Such is perhaps the case with Racine. His was an age of strict conventions, and perfection of form and appearances, and yet an age when fires, thinly veiled, raged under a veneer of calm, and the poet's imagination could sense them, and live them at levels where the real and the unreal merge into creations greater and truer than life. So we have that strange blend of Greek tragedy and Corneillean drama, of Greek passions lit by ruthless gods, and Christian hearts swept by forces which God's grace alone could have stopped. So we have Phèdre, Greek and Christian, pathetic and dramatic, sufferer and source of suffering, true to Greece and true to the seventeenth-century introspective analyses, true to the timelessness which is that of the great symbols of human life. We have plots, we have them in practically every one of Racine's plays, we have a plot in *Andromaque*, with sentimental and psychological motives, we have one in *Britannicus*, we have one in *Bérénice*, we even have one in *Phèdre*; we have dramatic interest, we wonder whether Thésée is dead or alive, whether Andromaque will choose either to remain faithful to her husband's memory or to save her son, yet we have also and in large measure pathos— the pathos of Phèdre, of Andromaque, of Bérénice, of all those whose fate, internally or externally actuated, is beyond their control. Above all, we have poetry—the heart-rending poetry of beings brought down to the bare bones of suffering, shorn of any shreds of human hope, face to face with the awe-inspiring realization that the Divinity stained by human sins is nevertheless the only refuge where the individual may find the peace of Eternity.

In the whole of French poetry there is nothing more moving than the extraordinary poetry which rises from these forlorn situations. With Racine we are back on the shores of Greece, at the foot of the Acropolis, or within sound of the waves, at Eleusis, and there we witness those moments in which men commune, through poetry, with the mysteries which fill their hearts. Strange as it may seem, the world of Racine is also the world of Shakespeare, the world in which man tries through poetry to reach mysteries which lie beyond him; it is the world of Hamlet, the world of Lear on the Heath, alone with his fool's wisdom and his broken heart; it is in the end the world of Prospero, the world where empyrean heights have been reached and men have at last calmly accepted the rains and the suns of heaven. Yet Racine, while being Greek, and a maker of

Eternity, is also French. He vigorously maintains the principles of the plot from which anything which is irrelevant is excluded. Love, the most fundamental of human passions, becomes the mainspring of his dramatic action, driving it forward, and giving it violence and pathos. Love and women are, in Racine, the anarchic forces, the founts of crime and destruction; yet they are also the causes of the most intense moments of life, of the moments which are the basis of our awareness of existence. Racine's progress, like Shakespeare's, is essentially that of a poet who moved from the uncertainties, doubts, and dramatic tensions of middle-life to the superb poetic flights of the end. There, plots, dramatic tensions, matter little. What counts is the poetry embodying the ebb and flow of souls face to face with supreme truth; in *Esher* and *Athalie* we are back to Greece, with choruses, music, décor, vagueness of place, lack of conflict, simplicity of plot and psychology, the whole resting above all on poetry born from the realization that our destiny is in God's hands.

Racine's plays, like Shakespeare's, have often suffered from being viewed from the exclusive angle of character and dramatic construction instead of from the angle of the wholeness of poetry. Of course, even if one looks at Shakespearean drama from these angles only, one can find enough qualities of greatness, for Shakespeare could impose the hallmarks of his genius on any material, and light the depths of the human soul; yet if we take only these vantage points of character and drama, there are many aspects of his great plays which we shall find rather difficult to accept and to enjoy, for the dramatic construction of not a few of his plays, including some of the greatest, is by accepted classical standards weak. *Hamlet*, if examined simply as drama, shows traces of the welding together of the plot and the action which form its substratum; but who can pause to think of this when carried away by its imaginative truth rising towards worlds which cannot be completely explored? The greatness is in the poetry which is the source of revelation and pathos, and we do not wait anxiously to know whether Hamlet will or will not kill the King: we do something different—we suffer the agonies of his puzzled mind and of the misery and death which it inflicts on him and on all those others who also do not deserve it. And what of the most Greek of Shakespeare's tragedies—*Lear*? Where is the drama, where is the suspense heightened from scene to scene, leading us to the expected, yet dreaded, conclusion? Nowhere. The fatal event, the source of all suffering, is at the beginning; it is no gods' fault, though it could be, it is described as a flaw in Lear's character. Still the mystery remains, and from that flaw, fount of all troubles, dreadful omen of things to come, all things develop in an atmosphere of intense suffering and of tragic pathos which is spread on a cosmic scale, and embraces life in all its forms, rising from the human to the transcendental in an awe-inspiring whole, which is the poem. What counts in Shakespeare as well as in Racine is the poem, not the drama, for they were first and foremost great poets—revealers of mysteries, and not architects, or masters of skilled, exciting, dramatic constructions. Racine has suffered too much from the kind of criticism which makes him the heir of Corneille, someone who continued and perfected a task which his predecessor had begun. He no doubt continued and perfected certain things, but first and foremost he expressed his genius within the conventions and the context of his time. It is in the compromise between those two things that lies his achievement, which expresses and transcends his time.

The differences between Racine and Corneille are profound and fundamental. A glance at what one may call their respective ' philosophies '—something which, in the case of poets more easily than in the case of philosophers, may be resolved into questions of attitudes to language—should throw light on them. Corneille identifies being and will: ' I will, therefore I am,' says the Corneillean hero. This identification of being and will, this acceptance of the idea of a choice which makes the being and gives him the awareness of his own existence, is now one of the main tenets of a certain form of existentialism. Corneille, of course, does not state implicitly or explicitly that the choice is compulsory, but in fact we cannot fail to realize that the Corneillean hero makes himself, by a conscious choice in a present which he makes as he knows it and wills it. That attitude is as old as social man; what is recent is the analysis of the motives which created it, but the gestures are old, they are certainly as old as Seneca and the Stoics; '*Je suis maître de moi comme de l'univers*,' says the Corneillean hero, echoing the ' I and I alone against the universe ' of the Senecan hero. As long as the *I*, the ego of the Corneillean hero, remains unbroken, no catastrophe can take place, nothing can shake the true existence of the being who can accept even death with a feeling of mastery, as the crowning glory of a life which has been willed from beginning to end. It is impossible not to note here how the psychological data in Corneille's plays are closely related to the philosophical views of Heidegger and Sartre, while one could find in Racinian psychology that pre-eminence of the ontological argument and that Pascalian despair which form the basis of Christian existentialism. The Corneillean hero, God-like in some ways, lives in the present, which is timeless and without past or future; he is the chosen moment, the expression of the will immanent and transcendent, continuously emerging from the nothingness which surrounds him. This insistence on the moment willed brings out two aspects of Corneille's drama which are closely connected with his age, the age of the end of the Renaissance and the age of Descartes. The moment of the will of the Corneillean hero is in some ways the intuitive moment of thought, which in Descartes unites creation and Eternity; in both cases we realize that we have moved away from the unbroken continuity in human time within the context of Eternity, of the Middle Ages, and that existence is no longer continuous, but has become a succession of willed moments, or intuitive flights which transcend the temporal. Man has risen in status to be more than a man, for, like an angel, he can go from higher points to higher points without intermediary; God, on the other hand, has diminished in stature and disappeared, leaving behind Him an immanent nature of which man is a part, a nature which, in its becoming, does not need Him, a nature in which man, through his will, can achieve immortality. In some ways we are back in a pagan world beyond Good and Evil.

Corneille is a poet, and what he makes with the words which are, or should be, his metaphysics, is what concerns us. Just as in his world there is nothing beyond man, in the same way there is nothing beyond his words; his words are all, a beginning and an end in themselves; they have no resonance in the past nor prolongations in the future, for there is no past or future for them; they do not link up with a mysterious and eternal reality; they are nothing else but themselves, and they live and die merely as words; they form the texture of the Corneillean hero who lives only by them; they have no revelatory power, for there is nothing to reveal; they are themselves in a naked violence which at times carries us away, and at certain moments leaves us unmoved. The poetry of Corneille is essentially rhetorical, and though there is good and bad rhetoric, rhetoric can never be placed on the same level as true poetry; it can never produce such rich and rewarding experiences in the reader or listener, for it does not involve the whole being of the creator. We somehow feel that Corneille's creations do not spring from the very depth of himself; they are not truly real, they have not been imaginatively lived, and therefore they are not completely convincing. Corneille was not a true poet, as Shakespeare or Racine were; he was a man endowed with a profound knowledge of the human soul and a dazzling verbal virtuosity, a virtuosity which leaves even Victor Hugo behind. He had gifts which are part and parcel of great poetry, but which are not enough to create it; he occupies in regard to Racine a position somewhat similar to that of Ben Jonson, or perhaps Chapman, in regard to Shakespeare. One may say in his favour that his conscious efforts to work within conventions enabled him to reach, with the means at his disposal, an excellence of drama which is on a higher plane than that of his two English contemporaries. For he was keenly aware of a truth which Byron later outlined in his foreword to *Sardanapalus* (1821): ' the author has in one instance attempted to preserve, and in the other, to approach, the " unities ", conceiving that with any very distant departure from them there may be poetry, but can be no drama '. Leaving out Shakespeare, it seems safe to say that conventions are safety barriers which enable those to walk who cannot fly.

The Racinian hero, in being Greek, is also essentially Christian; the fatalism of the Greeks becomes the ineluctable inner force which leads the being to its appointed end within

God's Will. With him we return to the soul whence the myths arose as projections and memories which go beyond man. The external compulsion of the Greeks has become the inner compulsion of the passions viewed from the Christian angle which links up Time and Eternity, and man and his end—God—in the moment of redeeming grace. Here we are back in existence in Time; everything—cognitive feelings, will, suffering—takes place in Time and yet has implications beyond Time, for cognition tends towards God. But the body is the centre, the intersection of Time and Eternity, the source of sin and suffering, and yet God-made, and therefore returning to God through the mystery of incarnation and redemption. This is the world of man stained by sin, but retaining the hope that he may rise to the Light. Hence the poignancy of the tragedies of Racine. The suffering is the knowledge of the separation from God's Will, a separation which is due to the awareness of sin. Hence the desperate longing for death, which, as in the case of Phèdre, will not immediately bring peace but which, once it is accepted as the unavoidable issue, implies the acceptance of God's Will and the eventual return to peace in oneness with God. Racine's heroes are Christians; they are parts of God's creation; they know that, apparently impelled by Fate, which is in fact original sin, they will do evil unless they are saved by God's Grace; and God Himself is perhaps somehow involved in that process, for evil seems to be inherent in creation; therefore we are face to face with the unfathomable terror of the being who fears that there may be no peace, not even in death, not even in the Divine. It is the terror of the being who fears that he may have stained the Divinity—the terror of Phèdre. Yet her death, freely accepted, implies her submission to the Eternal; it is indeed at the moment when she is about to lose light and life that she becomes suddenly aware of the true purity of light, and of sinlessness which is the Divine. Her awareness of sin and her submission to the Divine Will may be her salvation; in the end she is not explicitly blessed with God's Grace, but she has the truly Christian revelation of her past stained with evil and of her future separated from God; and at the very point of her self-willed death, in a final flash of her consciousness, she has the absolute knowledge of her situation, with all the suffering that it implies, and also with the glimmer of hope, implied by her last action, that her suffering may be the purgation which will bring her back into God's Will. She has at last discovered God and the unbearable knowledge of having offended Him, and therefore, with her past of sin and error, the present becomes a revelation of her decadence, and she leaps into the future with the hope that her death may bring her what she has never had in life—Divine Grace.

On the human plane knowledge is embodied in language, and language reveals to the Racinian hero the horror of an existence separated from God—his Source. That is why the action in Racine is not important; what matters is the knowledge of it through language. Why did the action take place that way? Because of a determinism which, in the Greek world, was external and in the Christian world is internal—lack of Divine Grace; but the results are the same—knowledge always follows the action, and comes, therefore, always too late. We have here an attitude to language completely different from that of Corneille. While Corneille uses language to enable the tragic hero to save himself, to release himself from the weight of the tragic action, and to try to maintain his ego intact for as long as possible, Racine uses language to show the hero the weight of his errors and his responsibility for the misery which he has spread round him, and therefore to make him realize that the only thing left for him is to die. For Racine absolute knowledge is death; in this belief he anticipates modern psychology, the poetry of Valéry and the hesitations of *La jeune Parque*. With Corneille poetry is the means of salvation of the self, and not a means to link the self with the great One. This poetry has no metaphysical ramifications; the words are instruments and an end in themselves; they are not the truth, the absolute knowledge which no human being can bear, but the means to save the human self. These differences imply two different conceptions of poetry, or rather a difference between real poetry and an extraordinary mastery of the dialectics of passions against passions or of passions against concepts, a mastery which can be one of the great attributes of poetry, but which is not the fundamental one.

Revelatory poetry alone can bring about that supreme confrontation between the individual self and the Great One, source of all selves—a confrontation which brings to the individual self the intuitive awareness of his separation (because of his errors and failings) from the Great One; that revelation of the isolation of the self attempting to live in contradiction with the indeflectible will, the spring of life, can be resolved only by the death of the self, a death which may or may not entail the physical death of the body. The nature of Corneille's poetry being different, the conflict lacks the metaphysical background which alone can bring poetry to heights beyond the human; the conflict remains on the human plane, the words are human instruments, they are the instruments of reason, conscious reason only, the reason which implies separateness, distinctiveness from the Source, and therefore the words are not revelatory and self-creative, but the termini of complex human experiences containing passions and thoughts analysed and lived through by the conscious process of speech. The words are, in Corneille, the means of exploring the action, of making it progress, and also the means of explaining it. A dramatic situation has been chosen, and the poet uses the words to unfold it. In Racine the words are *all*; the characters reveal themselves and their actions through the words; the actions are the result—the unavoidable result—of the words, or rather, the actions are unavoidable because of an inner compulsion whose causes are beyond us, and the words reveal what those actions are. Metaphysically, we can say: in the beginning was action, which revealed the word. Creation is God's action and word at the same time, for by being He makes Himself known, and He could be known only by being. All things are in God, but exist and are revealed only through Being, in Time. In God, action and thought are one and all; the word is part of God's action, but neither precedes it nor follows it; it is the action and it is the revelation, the knowledge of what is; man is God's action—the word made flesh; therefore the action, in order to be understood by man, must exist in Time, but metaphysically the *word* is *all*, thought and action at the same time.

In revelatory poetry, which is the only poetry which can

reach greatness, the word has all its metaphysical implications and is the action. In Shakespeare, for instance, we find the two ways of handling the words. The first, the Corneillean way, is responsible for a great deal of good rhetorical and dialectical verse and, like that of Corneille, bears the imprint of Senecan stoicism. The greater part of this type of verse is in the historical plays, in plays which exalt the will. The second mode, the mode of Racine, is the mode which is responsible for *Hamlet, Antony and Cleopatra, The Tempest,* etc. Of course, there is action in these plays; yet he does not subordinate his poetic genius to these actions and situations, but carries them on his wings, and utters words which reach into the very sources of these actions, and will from then on be their revelations. And it is when he gives words that magic revelatory power that he reaches the summits of poetry.

In the Elizabethan age and in the age of Corneille, Seneca's and Quintillian's works on rhetoric were widely read. Hamlet himself knew something of them, as is shown by his advice to the players. Corneille, the son of a lawyer, and a lawyer himself, was a man of the Renaissance, a contemporary of Chapman and of Ben Jonson. The aim of rhetoric being to persuade, it may take the form of a conscious effort combining words and gestures in order to create an emotive state which will win the reader or listener, or it may be a logical, cogent display of reasoning which cannot fail to carry conviction. It is an attempt to convey to the listener or reader a definite experience by means of overwhelming or winning over his judgment, therefore the experience of the listener or reader will not be creative, but will be imposed upon him by the poet; that experience will gain only a temporary acceptance, for as it has not been truly lived and re-created by the listener or reader, it will not become part of his experience; it will not be true knowledge—which is what true poetry should be—it will remain an inferior kind of poetry. The poetry will not rise from the event or the thing described in its simplicity or complexity, but will be given life with an aim in view, and both its morality and beauty will tend to be explicit and not implicit, as they should be.

It seems to me that the test of whether rhetoric is good or

bad lies in its power of conviction. If the author forgets himself, and uses his characters, or one of his characters, in order
to expound his own ideas, or if he allows the characters to
speak beyond the stage to the audience, then we have bad
rhetoric. If a character dramatizes himself unconsciously, or
if his words and gestures do not match the emotions or feelings
which he is seeking to convey, then we also have bad rhetoric,
for the words are no longer there in order to express a given
situation, but because the author, carried away by his verbal
skill, cannot resist a display of his virtuosity. In Corneille,
the characters have to be convincing in order that they should
convince both themselves and their friends and foes of the
necessity of their actions; they have to know what they will,
and the poetry is also willed. That means that Corneille
as a poet knew how to present poetically certain actions, and
was fully convinced of their necessity. In some of Shakespeare's
plays—the early historical ones—we have the same attitude:
the characters know what they want, and the requisite actions
are carried out in order to attain these aims. But with the
growth of his genius, we can see that Shakespeare's conception
evolved, that he passed from certitude, through the uncharted
land of incertitude which underlies the fundamental causes of
human actions, and which led him to the mastered calm and
the apparent simplicity of the characters of his last plays—
Miranda, Caliban, Ariel, Perdita, Imogen, etc.—plays in
which all doubts are resolved, all hesitation shed, all fields
explored, so that one may say with King Lear: ' Ripeness is
all '. The poetry of those plays, rising from the contingent,
leaves behind it the event or the thing which inspired it, and
reaches towards the absolute, sustained only by the impetus
of its initial force. We have here something similar to Dante's
last canto of *Il Paradiso,* in which the poetry is the final shaft
of light still bright after its source has already disappeared.
They are very rare, these moments when poetry is like the
rays still seen after the sun has set, they are the projection of
something beyond our world, glimmers of revelation. In
Shakespeare's great plays the poetry is revelatory. It seeks
to find the source of the catastrophes which shake men, and
it deals with situations so complex, so laden with human

suffering that the words cannot unravel them, and the poet who seeks through his poetry to explore them, at times succeeds in fusing the conflicts and contrasts which rage in his soul into lines whose inspiration bears the mark of illuminating finality.

The seventeenth century is the age of Descartes, the age which unifies the intuitive moment of thought with creation and eternity; that consciousness of the moment's existence revealed by thought destroys the continuity of human time, separates thought from things, and sets in motion a process of fragmentation of human life. Imagination can no longer apprehend life as a whole, and begins to lose its importance, giving way to analysis; and with imagination goes poetry. What remained was a polished, poetic diction, remote from integrated life, and which was only the shadow of the full-blooded force which filled the preceding age. Just as an extraordinary growth can exhaust the earth which gave it birth, in the same way great poetic geniuses can exhaust all the resources of the languages which they use. After Shakespeare and Milton, nobody could hope to use blank verse without summoning their great shadows; after Racine we had to wait for the Romantics, and above all for the symbolists, to open new fields to poetry. At the close of the seventeenth century the stars had reached their zenith, and man could bask in the brilliance of a light which shone on one of the most radiant moments of Western civilization. Yet society's divisions were widening, language had lost its metaphysical power, and poetry, fearing the inclemencies of the weather, had joined the powdered ladies and gentlemen who looked at trees and birds through window-panes; on the other hand, prose had grown to full maturity and, with prose, the age of reason, the growth of the novel, the advent of realism in the arts. Voltaire, La Grange-Chancel, Campistron, and Crébillon tried in vain to imitate Racine. The result was melodrama, with overworked plots, shallow psychology, pasteboard characters, and hollow rhetoric which had nothing to do with poetry. It is strange to think now that Voltaire's brilliant pieces of dialectics were considered, in his time, as the equal of Racine's masterpieces; it gives an idea of the age in which Voltaire lived, the age of reason and enlightenment, the age of the search for truth and belief in the improvement of the human condition. It was not, as has often been said, an age devoid of passions, but rather an age in which passions and emotions began to be divorced from reason entirely engrossed in the search for truth. That division could not but be fatal to poetry, because it no longer represented the whole man; it became didactic, rhetorical, and devoid of lyricism.

With *Athalie* tragedy and poetry disappeared from literature until the Romantic age. But the French Romantics were too concerned with the idea of trying to escape from the rules and conventions of seventeenth-century drama; as a result they were unable to appreciate the unique poetry of Racine; they thought that the freeing of drama from the shackles of the unities and the separation of genres would enable it to soar into poetry. Their ideal was Shakespeare, but they had not gone beyond the surface of Shakespeare's work, they had not understood the use of the grotesque in Shakespeare, they saw only the external expression of the emotion—the laughter— failing to realize that that kind of laughter which prepares us for greater flight is more unbearable than any terrifying grin; for it springs from even more profound emotional sources— the intuitive apprehension of nothingness. Above all, none of them had the kind of poetic genius which could probe the very sources of life, and their imaginative creations remained therefore inchoate, incoherent, incapable of having a life of their own. They gave us only the external aspects of things without the substance. They failed to see that pathos is not a matter of incidents and plots, but of situations which no human being can master. There are passages in Victor Hugo's theatre which are lyrical and convey a certain amount of pathos, but they are extremely few. His preoccupations lead him on a path previously followed by Voltaire. Like him he was too concerned with expressing his philosophy, which was, of course, very different from that of Voltaire, but which led him to use similar means; his rhetoric, contrasted with the cerebralism of Voltaire, is essentially emotional, but it remains nevertheless rhetoric, and not poetry, and his search for colourful situations, for striking historical events and plots led him away from tragedy into melodrama. Musset is the only Romantic writer who restored tragedy, or rather the tragic element, to the stage. We are of course very far from the tragic pathos of the Greeks or of the plays of Racine, yet although Musset was only a minor poet, he had a genuine lyrical gift, and a true sense of tragedy. His main theme, like Racine's, is love, and although he has neither the poetic power nor the psychological insight of Racine, his poetry succeeds sometimes in being the revelation of the feelings and forces which lead the characters to their end. The action is not a progression but is, as in tragedy, a centre from which everything radiates: therefore we have psychological unity. The mainspring of Musset's drama is the fatality of love; it is the source of misery and greatness, it is the mysterious force which, in spite of themselves, binds human beings to its laws and rules their lives, which sometimes end in disaster. We are not too far from the *ananke* of the Greeks.

By the middle of the nineteenth century, Romanticism seemed to have expended its force. A new age was being born, the age of machines, the age which showed more and more vividly the contrast between ideals and human misery, the age in which religion was still struggling under the rubble beneath which Robespierre, high priest of ' l'Etre Suprême ', had tried to bury it, the age in which the failure of social uprisings and revolutions led to the abandonment of the ideals which had guided them, and to the acceptance of Realism in the arts and in politics; the result was force in politics and materialism in thought, Bismarck and Karl Marx. It was the age of the evolutionist theories, of matter without mind, the age of Fourier and all the attempts to improve the human lot, the age of the application of scientific methods to everything, the age which, tired of the exuberance, the love of dramatic contrasts, and the intensity of feelings of the Romantics, decided to put an end to those ' errors ', by adopting a more realistic attitude towards the arts. This realistic attitude made itself felt in the theatre with the plays of Scribe and his followers, and it is an attitude which left no room for poetry. Yet those attempts were anything but successful.

The exuberance of language of the Romantics, the attempts made by the realists to use only words, images, and symbols which were universally accepted, led to two reactions which on the technical plane constitute the foundation of the symbolist doctrine. The first consisted in an attempt to re-intellectualize language and poetry, and the second in an attempt to renew the vitality of symbols and images and also to increase the subjectivity and the subtleness of language in order to try to encompass the greater complexity and some of the mystery of the poetic experience. These attempts to refine language and to give fulness and truth to artistic experience led to impressionism, pointillism, and surrealism in the arts, and produced a form of atomized realism which developed ' realism ' out of reality.

The great Romantic writers, from Chateaubriand to Victor Hugo and Lamartine, had all been concerned with, and had taken an active part in politics. This interest in politics is very often reflected in their works. René wore his heart on his sleeve and spent his life talking of the solitude of the poet, yet he could never keep away from the crowd, or rather, from courts and political arenas. It was Vigny who not only proclaimed the poet's solitude but also began to live that solitude in the silence of his Ivory Tower. The symbolists did not retire into the Ivory Tower, but politics were as alien to their art as was the scientific approach of the Realists, or the marmorean impersonality of the Parnassians. They were, above all, concerned with their own visions, their own experiences, which they sought to convey in their own way through a very personal language. Baudelaire retained some of the accepted symbols of the Church, but Mallarmé used symbols of his own personal choice, and such an extreme subjectivity in matter and form renders the apprehension of his poems rather difficult.

The second half of the nineteenth century is shadowed by the powerful genius of Wagner, whose influence was acknowledged by all the important symbolist writers. Verlaine said, *De la musique avant toute chose*; poetry for Baudelaire was the rhythmic creation of beauty, Mallarmé had said that ' the poet must see with his ears ', and constantly moves from concrete reality to the pure ideas which form the Platonic harmonies. For him the aim of the poem was not to inform but to suggest and to fuse reality into a fluid dream, and each object was for him the passing symbol of the idea, source of the object. That world of symbols was subordinated to a system of ideas ruled by laws which together constitute the Divinity, and Mallarmé looked upon himself as the priest of the mystery of the universe; at the same time he had, like Shelley, and later Valéry, a tendency to consider man as a fault in the absolute. He believed that the poet's task was to eliminate the contingent from things, to do away with creation—*le hasard*—and to return through words purified—having retained only the essence of things—to the Absolute. Mallarmé compressed his metaphors to the extreme limit of comprehension and relied entirely on the value of the word-image. ' Imagism ' may in some ways have begun with him. The word in his poetry is used more as an instrument of suggestion than as a means of description; it does not describe, but rather creates, the image or the hollow left by the image of the object; the word is thus used in the same way as musical notes. But the greatest and purest music is the music of silence, and for the poet and the composer the problem must therefore consist in how to find a way by which the poetry and the music shall be born not from the words or the notes, but from the intervals between the notes and from the hollow left by the object which the word will have annihilated, leaving behind its quintessential image.

Symbolism in its various aspects—expressionism, surrealism, etc., symbolism meaning first and foremost a poetry of suggestion and complexity—remains the most important aspect of the poetry of our time. The first symbolist poets—Baudelaire, Rimbaud, Mallarmé—did not write for the theatre. It is only the post-symbolists—W. B. Yeats, T. S. Eliot, Maeterlinck, Claudel, and others—who turned their attentions towards the stage. Between the two waves of symbolism lies a renewed upsurge of materialism in various forms, and at the same time a great revival of the theatre. That revival centres mostly round the names of Ibsen and Shaw. Although he wrote mainly in prose, Ibsen had great poetic gifts; he introduced in the theatre rules of intellectual integrity and positive cohesion which gave his personages the consistency and pathos of real human beings. His realism was neither a photograph of life nor an overwhelming concern with its stark aspects, as was the case with Zola; starting from life, he went beyond it. His diagnoses, his laying bare of society's ills, are those of a man who was more than a clinician, a man who was endowed with the power to relate those temporal failings to the perennial, and to give truth a well-nigh unbearable glare.

The movement towards realism in the theatre initiated by Ibsen spread to all countries and to all aspects of theatrical production. Naturalistic writing, naturalistic acting, naturalistic scenery invaded the theatre, and were carried to extraordinary lengths. Among the playwrights who followed in the wake of Ibsen none was endowed with his poetic gift. The realism of Zola or of Henri Becque tends to confine itself too much to the stark and gloomy aspect of human life, yet it did break away from the ideal of *la pièce bien faite* and *la pièce à thèse* which had dominated the French stage since Scribe and the younger Dumas. But playwrights and producers were not long in realizing the danger of naturalism and in opposing it vigorously. In this country William Poël and Granville-Barker, Gordon Craig, and others set about reforming the theatre and restoring poetry to its pre-eminence on the stage. There are of course marked differences between the latter and the first two, but they all agreed on one main point— that what was important was the text, and not the various contraptions which weighed more and more heavily on drama. ' Realistic scenery is anathema ', said Gordon Craig; ' the stage is an artificial place in which the natural looks wrong as an artificial flower looks wrong in a garden.' It is essential to preserve the unity of the theme, and not to get lost in naturalistic scenery. Of course, Gordon Craig also said that the producer was the one supreme artist in the theatre, and that all the others—dramatists, actors, etc.—should be entirely controlled by him. That view does not coincide with those of William Poël and Granville-Barker, who were for team work; they were above all interested in the importance of the text, and they were against cuts and arrangements being made to suit personal tastes. In that connection, it is worth noting the attempts now being made to return to a more Shakespearean atmosphere with the apron stage and uninterrupted acting.

D   [43]

In France, where artistic traditions are deep-rooted, Ibsen's influence was less strongly felt and lasted less long than elsewhere. In 1887 André Antoine founded the ' Théâtre Libre ', whose primary aim was to encourage new experiments in drama. That theatre has often been described as naturalistic, and the term is appropriate, for in order to produce non-commercial plays Antoine reduced the scenery to the minimum, but that scenery was realistic to the point of having real butcher's meat on the stage. What is interesting is that when this movement started, France thereby became the pioneer of movements which sprang to life in Germany, England, and in Ireland, and that because it was a non-commercial theatre, it produced and encouraged poetic drama. The ideals of Antoine were not those of Jacques Copeau, who was among other things firmly opposed to the naturalistic school, but they had one point in common, which was that the play was judged on its intrinsic merits as a play, and not as a good commercial proposition. With the ' Théâtre Libre ', we are right at the beginning of the period which can be described as modern. It is the period which begins with Maeterlinck and Rostand and continues with Claudel, Supervielle, and Henri Ghéon, and with one aspect of poetic drama which is more typical of France than of any other country, and more of our time than of any other time, and that is the drama of all those who, like Giraudoux, Cocteau, Anouilh, Obey, and others, make use of ancient Greek myths and legends.

There is very little poetry and tragic feeling in what is described as the poetic drama of Maeterlinck. The so-called poetry of Maeterlinck's plays is generally reduced to a matter of devices, conventions, and worn-out themes; the philosophy is vague, undigested, and above all untransmuted into the dramatic characters, who ought to have a life of their own. The mainsprings of dramatic action and tension are lacking, the characters are generally the prey of mechanistic forces, and therefore they do not arouse our sympathy. Maeterlinck's main failure is as a poet, for had he been a poet he might have poured into *Pelléas et Mélisande*, for instance, the dramatic pathos which can move an audience witnessing the undeserved suffering of noble hearts; he would have given us not vague pseudo-philosophical statements, simple allegories and idea-emotions, but imaginative creations which would have had a life of their own and would have conveyed the experience of a philosophy detached from the life and thoughts of their creator.

Rostand, though not a major poet, is an important one from the special place he occupies in French poetic-drama. He is not only a kind of reaction to Symbolist poetry, but a combination of the two strains—idealism and realism—which, at the end of the nineteenth century, were contending for pre-eminence, and also the representative of a great tradition in French poetry: I mean rhetorical poetry. *Cyrano* is a heroic comedy in verse, and therefore we cannot expect to find in it the kind of revelatory poetry we find in *Othello, King Lear,* or *Phèdre.* The aims of the poet are here limited but clear, and the speech in *Cyrano* is a development of character and a building up of dramatic tension. The dramatic action is on the whole sustained, and there are scenes of true dramatic and poetic beauty; for instance, the marvellous tirade on noses, with the reply to the Vicomte—a brilliantly developed metaphor which is dramatic and which produces, through the self-irony of the main character, a heightening of sensitiveness to which one can hardly refuse the name of poetry. Rostand was essentially a dramatist, and when he was successful as such, his rhetoric was more effective than Victor Hugo's or Baudelaire's, who were much greater poets. The problem is different with Claudel. Here we are once more face to face with the work of a major poet, and a poet who is first and foremost a poet-dramatist who restored poetry to the stage.

II

BEGINNING

Tête d'or

' TÊTE D'OR ', Claudel's first important work for the stage, is a poem about the failure of human wishes and ambition. It points to the morality that all hopes which do not look beyond the earth are condemned to bankruptcy and cannot prevail over the power which controls all things:

> Voici que l'homme a terminé sa suprême entreprise, tout est fini.
> Et il ne prévaudra point
> Contre la Puissance qui maintient les choses en place.

(p. 277)

So speaks one of the minor characters, who sometimes act as a chorus, summing up and explaining the action; the play closes with these words:

> Et notre effort, arrivé à une limite vaine,
> Se défait lui-même comme un pli.

It is divided into three parts. The first part opens with Simon Agnel burying his wife in a field. His childhood friend, Cébès, recognizes him, and it is to him that Simon Agnel explains how, having left his native village, lured by the attraction of wide horizons, he has now returned home to bury the woman who had given him her faith and who has just died. After the burial, and Simon Agnel's lamentations over the grave, Cébès asks him for his help and protection, and the first part ends in a very exalted atmosphere of forced symbolism, with Simon Agnel's blood falling over Cébès' head as the seal of his promise to protect and guide him.

The introduction to a play should constitute the exposition of the forces which knit the plot together and carry it to its *dénouement;* it should introduce us to the characters, and give us an idea of their probable reactions and of the actions which they may carry out. It should present us with the seeds of the passions and ideas which will force men and women into situations and through actions which will excite our interest in mounting suspense towards a *dénouement* feared and yet expected, and this *dénouement* will solve all the problems, and all the questions which have been raised. Yet at the end of the introduction to *Tête d'or* we know hardly anything worth knowing about the main character and the chief motives of his actions; we have not the faintest idea of the course that the characters which have been introduced to us may take or of the kind of *dénouement* which may befall them. We are made aware that Simon Agnel is perturbed by Promethean dreams and visions of Alexander's glory, but we cannot find any explanation of what urges him forward; all we know is that he feels that he is a man of destiny born to accomplish great things. This vague prelude does not contain any dramatic element, any suspense and excitement, any tragic element or any source of the pathos born from the sight of undeserved and unavoidable suffering.

In the second part we learn that we are in a certain kingdom threatened by barbarians, and that its salvation rests in the hands of a young man called Tête d'or, a kind of god of war, who electrifies the cowards, and who brings back hope to all those who, before, knew only despair. The Court is spending the night in vigil waiting for news, while the fate of the kingdom is being decided by arms. At dawn a messenger arrives, bringing happy tidings: victory has been achieved. Soon afterwards Tête d'or arrives, just in time to witness the death of Cébès, who is carried away by a mysterious disease which, on the symbolical level on which the play unfolds, looks very much like the death of certain aspects of Tête d'or's personality, a willed death at that, a partial suicide, a destruction of certain of his selves which Tête d'or now decides to leave behind him. Cébès' death at dawn marks the beginning of a new life for Tête d'or, who reveals himself as the superman who wishes to mould the universe according to the design of his ego. He wants undisputed mastery over all things and beings. Therefore he kills the reigning King, drives away his daughter, the Princess, and assumes power.

In the third part we have at last some definite geographical indications: we are in the Caucasus. Tête d'or has subdued Europe; he is now on the last lap of his victorious march forward, for he is at the gates of Asia: if he succeeds he will have conquered the world. The fugitive Princess is also in that most fateful part of the world, and she is discovered by a deserter, who insults her and then crucifies her. The rumour reaches the camp that Tête d'or has died, the truth is that when his army fled, Tête d'or threw himself upon the enemy, and when wounded his cry rallied his men to victory. On hearing the rumour of Tête d'or's death, his friend Cassius commits suicide. After which we still have a long Promethean scene. Before dying, Tête d'or discovers the Princess nailed to a tree; he crawls towards her and liberates her, pulling out the nails with his teeth. After that he falls back exhausted, the Princess tells him that she loves him, and he dies in her arms; she, too, dies soon after.

The play contains no dramatic action with tension mounting towards a solution, nor are the characters who *will* the actions locked up in them in an inevitable way. What we have here is a succession of tableaux or events in which the main character is involved, and a symbolism which relates him to various extraordinary individuals, ranging from the great warriors of History to the Redeemer of mankind. This is a play of ideas, the ideas which were always astir in Claudel's mind and which will remain, to the end of his career as a playwright, the foundation of many of his dramas. The play is not situated in time or space, and even the indication that the third act takes place in the Caucasus is more symbolical than real; it merely confers certain attributes on the hero, it makes him partake of the dreams of some of the greatest figures of mankind, from Alexander to Napoleon, and it brings upon him, or rather it brings out of him, reflections of the most moving visions in the life of Man—Christ, Prometheus, Moses. From the very beginning of the play, when Tête d'or is still Simon Agnel, he seems to be more than a man; he feels in himself the restlessness which led Columbus to discover new lands, and the force which swept Moses ahead; he speaks with a voice which comes from beyond himself and uses a kind of imagery which associates him more and more with the ' Redeemer '. The end of Part One—the scene between Cébès and Simon Agnel—is both apocalyptic in its exultation and prophetic utterances, and certainly apocryphal in its obscurities:

> Pour moi qui t'ai tenu, Majesté, le moment est venu que j'ai pu
> dire : J'ai assez !
> Que ce lieu où un Roi me donna son sang,
> Que ce tournant de chemin soit marqué d'une pierre et appelé
> d'un nom !
>
> (p. 47)

says Cébès, whose relationship to Simon Agnel is difficult to assess. He seems to be Simon Agnel's other self, but whatever he is, he is extremely confused. Nevertheless the scene, though dramatically difficult to follow, does not lack poetic power. In spite of the overstressed exultation and the fulsome literary romanticism of the end, it is one of the most poetic scenes in the play.

Claudel has that fresh and natural vision of things which belonged to primal man or to the childhood of man; he sees things in images, and he sees things as they are, without any intellectual sophistication, and as part of the immutable ways of Nature. With him we are back to the *oneness* of man in the Middle Ages. There is no division between the spiritual and material worlds, the body is not spirited away into a vague Platonic world, but described in accurate, even gruesome or forceful images which have a stark Rabelaisian and Villonesque realism. Claudel possesses sometimes, but unfortunately not often enough, to a high degree that ' exact, sensuous imagination ' praised by Goethe. He can give us clearly defined, concrete images of things. From the beginning he shows himself to be a poet on a great scale. The replies of Simon to Cébès, ending in the invocation to the tree, show the wide range of the poet's imaginative vision. That majestic invocation to a tree, difficult to quote in extracts, reminds one in many ways of Coleridge's poem *Hymn before sun-rise*:

> O dread and silent mount! I gazed upon thee,
> Till thou, still present to the bodily sense,
> Didst vanish from my thought: entranced in prayer
> I worshipped the invisible alone.

[49]

In both cases we have remarkable examples of the loss of the self or subject into the object, which is the true poetic knowledge, and at the same time an example of the reconciliation of Plato and Kant as adumbrated by Schopenhauer. While one may apply Goethe's definition to the poetry of Claudel, one should nevertheless bear in mind the fact that the word ' exact ', which for Goethe implied not only a realistic and quasi-scientific precision, but also a kind of Apollonian serenity and control, is not valid for Claudel. He is no Apollonian genius, and if any reference to Greek mythology should be made, it is Dionysus' name which should be summoned and not Apollo's, for Claudel has indeed the exuberance and at times the prophetic frenzy of the god of vines. There are moments when the poet gets drunk with words, hollow rhetoric, and bombastic speeches, as in the scene when Tête d'or kills the King and takes the crown, and sometimes speaks like God Himself or like somebody directly inspired by God. When we are faced with such moments, in straightforward poetry or in drama, we cannot but feel repelled by the violent dogmatism and triumphant tone which precipitate poetry or character into bad rhetoric.

If one cannot fail to be profoundly impressed by Claudel's imagination and his power to give life to things or feelings in moving and concrete, though at times, earthy images:

> Plus seul que l'enfant tué par sa mère et qu'elle enterre sous le fumier avec
> Les assiettes cassées et les chats morts dans la terre pleine de gros vers roses!
>
> (p. 223)

we realize also that his triumphant dogmatism makes it rather difficult for him to allow his dramatic characters to live a life of their own. Tête d'or is obviously the kind of hero that the author wants to present to us; he is not part of a drama; he does things, but he does them for the sake of a demonstration willed by the author. He is the solitary genius, the Moses round whom everything he loves dies; he is the superman, the Nietzschean hero, whose ambition drives him forward to deeds which did not frighten another famous, ambitious man— Macbeth. In fact, the allusions to the latter seem in one or two cases clear enough. The death of the King, the bludgeoning of various people with the dead King's blood, have the symbolical value expounded in *The Golden Bough*, but dramatically they are not convincing. Tête d'or, like so many of Claudel's creations, gives the impression of an extraordinary being, a force of Nature, going through a forest of symbols, pulling them down, and piling them up in an heteroclyte yet grandiose construction in which there are many patches of great beauty; the materials are there, but what is lacking is the serenity which orders things into an harmonious, integrated whole. Just as in a poem images, metaphors, and rhythms must be congruent to the theme, or to the emotion or emotions underlying the theme, in the same way we expect to find in a play that congruence of characters and of traits within characters which constitutes the necessary organic oneness. Claudel's powerful imagination ranges far and wide, and is loaded with suggestiveness; Tête d'or seems to contain in himself all the various aspects of a prominent individual. He seems to be related to countless great personages who have at some time or another in history walked upon the earth, and even more than that, he sometimes sounds like God Himself; at other moments he is St. John the Baptist, shaking his golden locks

> Par ces cheveux
> Splendides, imprégnés par l'Aurore, toison trempée du sang le la
>   Mère, indice de la condition ingénue,
> Voile d'or que je soulève avec les mains!
>
> (p. 249)

Or again he is the great war leader, Alexander or Napoleon, marching eastwards to the conquest of the world, or perhaps he is a member of the Society of Jesus, who has the great principles of St. Ignatius at heart and is ready to fight for the Church Triumphant. He takes us to the door, the last door:

> Voici le seuil qui sur le Nord éternel est ouvert et le côté par où le
>   soleil arrive,

somewhere in the Caucasus, near the rocks where Prometheus died because he tried to reveal the secrets of the gods to men, or beyond the earth with the heroes of *Paradise Lost*, on the very threshold of heaven:

[51]

CASSIUS: Je vois l'étendue de la Terre!

LE MAITRE-DES-COMMANDEMENTS: Tourne-toi vers l'Est saint!

CASSIUS: La terre est comme un tapis étendu! Et au loin il y a un brouillard obscur.

LE MAITRE-DES-COMMANDEMENTS: Regarde, ô Roi, et prends, car tout cela est à toi.

Et la terre est à toi, comme un champ dont on a mesuré l'étendue.

(p. 259)

and this Dantesque ascension continues higher and higher:

Afin que nous gravissions la dernière marche et que de l'Asie
Nous conquérions l'énorme Autel!

(p. 259)

Then, in that indefinable apocalyptic setting, we are back again to the image of Christ, brutalized and crucified, represented by the Princess who, insulted by the deserter, endures nobly and rises above the human, imploring God from a situation strongly reminiscent of Calvary. The army which is fighting in these empyrean heights is the army of Jesus or of St. Ignatius, and the symbols on its banners are closely related to the Saviour's, whose love rises to God, and whose outstretched arms encompass the universe; we are at the heart of the Bible:

Certes tu verras le Roi du monde régner, mais tu n'as pas vu ce
que nous vîmes!
La terreur et l'éblouissement marchent devant lui . . .

(p. 266)

and the ' King of Men ' is struck to death by the sins and failings of humanity; yet his death will not have been in vain, for death, like the Great Death, is his victory. But before he dies the cycle must be completed, the parable explained; St. Thomas the surgeon comes and puts his finger in one of the wounds, and Tête d'or undoes the dressings of his wounds which speak out in blood in the Shakespearean language of Julius Caesar, and the *dénouement* is completely forced and therefore false; as false as the ' I am charmed ' of Tête d'or or the final arraying of the Princess in her majestic regalia.[1]

---

[1] Claudel loves liturgy, majestic ceremonies, and symbolic actions and pronouncements; he loves strange mixtures of ancient or exotic civilizations

That wide range of suggestiveness only throws into relief the great poetic power of Claudel, and also his failure as a dramatist. I mean, of course, his failure in this play, for when Claudel succeeds, as he has sometimes done, in controlling the various aspects of his genius, he produces outstanding plays, such as *Partage de Midi*, *La jeune fille Violaine*, and others. By the time those plays came, the impetuous torrent had reached the broad plain, and the original force, increased by all the tributaries of years of experience, had also acquired majesty and order. *Tête d'or* contains, side by side with striking poetry, passages of sheer bombast and unbearable rhetoric. Like his illustrious predecessor, Victor Hugo, with whom he has so much in common, Claudel sometimes shows a singular lack of critical judgment and a deficiency of taste which, in spite of extraordinary gifts, seems to imply a certain vulgarity of character. *Tête d'or* is more an epic than a play, but whatever word one may use to describe it, it is the work of a man who already shows the portents of a major poet.

---

with modern times. In a similar way, his style mixes Biblical and archaic expressions with very modern Parisian speech, as in the course of the dialogue between the deserter and the Princess. The lack of concreteness of these very unusual names and titles which increase vagueness—Cassius, Tête d'or, Le Suprême-Préfet, Le Pédagogue, l'Opposant, Le Maître-des-commandements, etc.—and their speeches, which vary from the monologue to the solemn prophetic utterances of visionary beings, all tend to plunge the reader in a dream world very remote from reality.

III

EARLY PLAYS

La Ville

As with *Tête d'or*, in *La Ville* we have no geographical localization of the action, yet the time can only be that of the industrial age, with social and economic problems coming to the front, and with prospects of the ' great Revolution ' about to take place.

In the First Act we have a town, without a name, and the first person we meet is Isidore de Besme, a scientist, who is the master of that town. His brother, Lambert de Besme, is interested in politics. We see Lambert de Besme in conversation with a strange nihilistic revolutionary called Avare, who seems to believe only in death and destruction, and who appears as the instrument of divine vengeance destined to destroy this corrupt town. Soon afterwards Avare goes away, leaving Lala, to whom Lambert offers his love; she accepts. They go to feed the fish in the park, and while they are there Isidore de Besme and the poet Cœuvre arrive. In the course of a magnificent dialogue both explain their conception of the universe and their views of life. Besme, who has a feeling for poetry, partly understands what Cœuvre tries to say, and Cœuvre tells him of his worries and doubts. Then come Lala, Lambert de Besme, and some delegates from the town. A complete change takes place in Lala, who throws herself at the feet of Cœuvre and declares that she loves him. Cœuvre accepts her as his wife. The Second Act takes place a long time after the first. Many things have happened—work has ceased in the town and Lala has left the poet Cœuvre. The first scene is set in a graveyard, where we find Lambert de Besme busy digging his own grave. He is soon joined by Lala, then by Avare, and the three of them have a long discussion about social questions, ranging from workers' conditions to the place of women in society. The debate is widened when Isidore de Besme and Cœuvre arrive.

Lambert, having said what he has to say, lies down in his waiting grave. Lala vaticinates about the future city, then Isidore de Besme, after a moving confession, leaves Cœuvre and goes to face death in the insurrection which is taking place.

The Third Act contains three main events—Avare's departure, Cœuvre's return, and the disappearance and return of Lala. Avare the revolutionary gives way to the leader of the future—Ivors, the son of Cœuvre, the poet, represents the creative mind, and Lala the eternal feminine. Cœuvre returns converted, with all the pomp of religion behind him. At the end Lala also returns, and, in spite of her failings, is accepted as the woman necessary to the life of the community.

Such is the bare outline of the play; as can easily be seen, there is neither a tragic force leading the protagonists to their doom, nor the dramatic tension and suspense arising from a well-knit plot and logical development of characters. The town is any town, it is the essential concept of a town, an abstraction which fits well within Claudel's expressionism. The characters are not true human beings, but projections of the poet's mind reflecting problems which preoccupy him; they are stylized into types. There is action, such as the rebellion in the town, but again this is reduced to essential structural lines, and is in no way dramatic, nor is it part of a sequence of events which follow one another in an inevitable way. On the contrary, we seem to be in the midst of a random life. Characters come and go, feelings and situations change, and the only woman of the play passes from one man to another for no other reason but the whim of the creative mind who pulls the strings and has conceived her more as a symbol of certain aspects of womanhood than as a real woman, with a heart and mind of her own.

A good deal of what has been said about *Tête d'or* applies also to *La Ville*. It is, on the whole, an excellent piece of writing, but it is certainly not drama; it is too obviously the statement of some of Claudel's conflicting beliefs and the record of an experience which is the crux of his life—I mean his conversion. But the whole thing has not been successfully objectified, the characters have no real life; they are only symbolical representations of certain ideas or certain aspects of Claudel's

[55]

personality. Besme, for instance, is not a man, but the spirit of science; he represents that aspect of extreme rationalism which leads to inhumanity; before dying he realizes the unsolvable mysteriousness of things, but it is too late for him, for then he can only die. Avare is the nihilistic revolutionary possessed with the urge of destruction. Lala is the woman, that aspect of Nature which represents the elemental aspect of life, the complement which man needs. She is the central element of the play, for she compels the poet to love and to know the joy of love, and she gives birth to the Prince who is to create the new city. Cœuvre, the poet, is the most clearly drawn character of the play. He is an obvious projection of Claudel. He speaks in words which we shall find again in *Cinq grandes odes* and in *L'art poétique*, and above all he re-enacts for us the conversion of Claudel.

The play lacks a central theme, and there is no dramatic progression, yet it contains, side by side with long passages of diffuse, repetitive argumentation, splendid passages of poetry; we find most of these, as is to be expected, in the part of Cœuvre. His replies to Besme the atheistic unbeliever, and to Lala, at the end of the First Act, are among the best poetry that Claudel has ever written. One cannot quote in extracts, and one needs to read the whole passage, beginning with: *O Besme, pour comprendre ce que je suis* . . . down to *Excommunié de quelle foi?* to find one of the most moving statements ever made by any poet about the meaning of poetry. Then, following the invocation to the moon, which seems to me stilted and slightly forced, we have a beautiful dialogue between Lala and the poet, magnificent poetry which already foretells *Partage de Midi*:

Je te salue dans ton voile.
Mais puisque je ne puis te voir, je te pèserai. Certes tu es lourde et pesante,
Et c'est à peine si je puis soulever tes pieds de la terre et voici que je prends charge de toi.
Voyez, ô vous tous qui m'entourez, hommes et femmes,
Et vous, assistance plus antique, arbres, toit des branches, voyez!
Et vous, ô cercle le plus large,
Cieux! étoiles
Qui tout à l'heure vous êtes allumées dans l'air blanc là-haut,

Comme quelqu'un qui couche dans une ferme, le matin entend
    au-dessus de lui que le peuple des colombes s'est réveillé!
Et toi, hiérophante,
Qui sur le bord où tu vas disparaître te tiens debout, la torche
    levée!
J'ai pris cette femme, et telle est ma mesure et ma portion de la
    terre.

(p. 446)

We cannot help being carried on the wave of those majestic
rhythms which rise and fall with the discovery of new emotional
fields.

    The poet realizes what Valéry fully realized only at the end of
his life in *Mon Faust*, that life can be apprehended only by living,
but never in the abstract, in its essence:

                            . . . Et c'est pourquoi,
Familiarisé au commerce des forces profondes,
J'avais projeté substituer à la connaissance le contact de surprendre
    l'Être dans son opération, combinant tel piège.
Je mêle cette pensée à l'obscurité de la Mort.

(p. 468)

    That thought comes to Besme too late, but whoever believes
in God's wisdom and in His grace sees things as they are, and
wants neither to know what is beyond them nor to change them;
he accepts without questioning whatever is the expression of the
unchangeable Will. Cœuvre says so to Lala and Avare with
all the force and beauty that a poet like Claudel can place at
the service of a cause in which he believes, and Avare replies in
rhythms and images which have a cosmic grandeur and are
comparable with the best of Victor Hugo:

Qu'avez-vous à vous étonner et à craindre?
Si la terre tremble dans l'épaisseur de sa masse,
Si la suture du ciel claque dans un coup de tonnerre, si l'Océan
    emporté par le ras-de-marée
Déracine ses caps et roule l'une sur l'autre ses îles comme des
    barriques,
Qui s'étonnerait que cette mer humaine d'âmes et de sang
Se mit un jour à bouillir et fit péter la paroi
Des réservoirs où vous essayez de la contenir, alors que l'heure est
    venue et que Mars entre au Lion?

(p. 465)

[57]

Claudel can pass from sensuous images and prophetic language such as:

> Que les étoiles se cachent, que le soleil se couvre d'un sac! . . .

to the logical precision of legalistic language, as when he expounds economic and political doctrines:

> Tout effort qui a le désir pour mobile suppose la satisfaction pour terme:
> Toute satisfaction est individuelle, tout terme est immobile.

Side by side with such a style we have samples of the most up-to-date Parisian slang: *loupiot, gosse,* etc.

In conclusion one may say that *La Ville* is neither drama nor tragedy, nor is it by any means a good play, yet it contains some of Claudel's best poetry, lines which will no doubt last as long as French literature.

Le Repos du Septième Jour

The action takes place in China, the most perfect Empire on earth, a vast, harmonious construction centred on the Emperor—God's image on earth. Yet, in spite of the Emperor's wisdom, strange things take place in that Empire: the living have no peace, the dead have left their graves and haunt them. The Emperor consults the hero, first father of the Empire—Hoang-Ti—and as he cannot obtain any reply from him, he decides to go down among the dead and to find out for himself the cause of the trouble. Here we have an atmosphere of tragedy, with forces beyond men's control, overwhelming them and disturbing their human happiness. The Emperor, the consciousness and soul of his people, endures great moral suffering, and is ready for self-sacrifice. Here we have pathos, and a vision of life on the metaphysical plane with the strange admixture of the living and the dead, and the supernatural elements which determine the action of the Emperor.

In the Second Act the journey of the Emperor through Hell contains the exposition of Claudel's theology in sometimes epic, sometimes simply descriptive poetry which is neither tragic nor

dramatic. We are on the metaphysical plane at the very
sources of Good and Evil.

The Third Act maintains the symbolical atmosphere of the
second. In the absence of the Emperor, the power which held
the Empire together has broken down, and this has brought
about a state of complete chaos. At this moment the Emperor
reappears, Christ-like, armed with the redemptory faith which
will restore peace among men. After having delegated his
authority to his son, he retires to a mountain, which seems to be
a kind of purgatory, and there he will devote the remainder of
his life to intercessory prayer in order to bring about the Kingdom of God on earth.

Le Repos du Septième Jour, which in some ways continues and
concludes *Tête d'or* and *La Ville,* is much less of a drama. There
is, as we have noted, a certain amount of pathos in the
Emperor's plight and in his meeting with his mother; there is
sometimes an atmosphere of tragedy; but, on the whole, human
passions appear only as extremely faint reflections of the fundamental problem of Good and Evil. The *dramatis personæ* are
really the Emperor of China and God, or rather, in the end,
Claudel himself, in the exultation of his newly found religious
plenitude. Therefore there is no drama, although we have at
times tragic pathos and good dramatic poetry forming part of a
poem which is, on the whole, on a high level. Somehow one
cannot help being reminded of Dante. The Emperor has not
lost his way in a dark wood, but something similar has happened
to him. The harmony of his Empire, of which he is a kind of
supra-human centre, has been broken. The dead cannot rest,
because of the sinful behaviour of the living, and they therefore
render life quasi-impossible. The Emperor decides to plunge
into the underworld and to find out the roots of the trouble.
We are back into the *Inferno* and into the atmosphere of Dante's
theology—we have the circles, we have the various guides, and
we have an explanation of sin and evil which compares with
Dante's metaphysics. The first step into sin is that of Paolo
and Francesca: *la douceur de faire le mal,* a form of evil which can
be refined only by the fire which is God's love. There is no
need to press the parallel between the two poets further;
sufficient to say that the Emperor, like Dante, finds his Beatrice,

E   [59]

the angel of the Empire, who leads him to the heights, and imparts to him the Divine Wisdom which can enable him to save his people. The Emperor returns to earth Christ-like, his sceptre transformed into a cross, his face made unrecognizable by leprosy, and filled with the faith which has come from the West and will save his people. He lays down his life with the certitude that he has brought the Kingdom of God on to the earth.

This is a poem which contains passages of striking beauty. The scene between the Emperor and his mother is very moving poetry, with penetrating rhythms and subtle texture, and the pathos of the scene is undeniable. The long scene with the Daemon, packed with metaphysical arguments, shows Claudel's visionary power and the depth of his thought; at the same time it shows clearly enough why he is not on the same level as Dante. He lacks the clearness of vision, crispness of diction, and rhythmic harmony which carried Dante to the summits. Claudel's visions, however impressive, remain confused, apocalyptic, and are at times expressed in abstract terms and with a tendency to repetition; he cannot control his wealth. In Dante we have simple words, but words which image, and concision and concreteness are amongst his main assets. Still, there are very few poets who call Dante to mind. The scene between the angel of the Empire and the Emperor, and above all the alternate song of the new Emperor and the Recitant at the end of the poem, are beautiful poetry.

So ends this liturgical pageant in the shadow of the Cross; it is probably Claudel's most profoundly religious poem, a poem pervaded with feelings of holiness and joy which show the timelessness of Christ.

L'Échange

Here the action is localized in time and space; it takes place on the East coast of the U.S.A. in our time. The First Act situates the main protagonists of the drama and knits the plot. On one side we have Louis Laine and Marthe, on the other we have Léchy Elbernon and Thomas Pollock Nageoire. We are plunged at once into an atmosphere which does not lack psychological truth and prepares us for what may happen.

The characters clearly contain elements which are bound to conflict and to produce a catastrophe. Louis Laine is a restless young man who cannot bear the weight of any ties, however light. Is his Indian blood the cause of his rebelliousness and predatory instincts, or is he a man whose inherent romanticism has never succeeded in reconciling social restrictions with the freedom of the primal instincts? We cannot decide. The fact is that as soon as we meet him we realize that he does not want to possess anything, or to be possessed by anybody, yet he is married, bound to a woman, Marthe, who loves him and believes in possession. Marthe represents the old world, with its settled ways, its acceptance of discipline, its beliefs in the spirituality of the land where we have been born and where we have grown up. She has the calm devotion of women used to waiting for years by their lonely firesides for the return of their men, and she belongs to that company of women who, if those men do not return, are prepared to wear black until the end of their lives. She believes that once she has given her pledge before God, nothing can free her from her decision. Thomas Pollock Nageoire is a business man of the new world, a man whose only fixed standard in life is money. He has obviously, from the beginning, an interest in Marthe. His concubine, Léchy Elbernon, is an actress, a woman ever in search of new sensations, and she has already cast her eyes on Louis Laine. This exposition definitely contains the conflicting elements endowed with explosive force which will produce the *dénouement*.

In the Second Act Louis Laine wants to leave his wife, and tells her of his decision. Marthe answers in a most moving speech. Léchy comes to Laine's rescue, tells Marthe of their relations, and encourages him to come with her. Marthe agrees to leave Laine.

Act Three begins with Marthe's moving meditation by the sea. Léchy comes in drunk; she insults Marthe, and tells her that if she wants to save her husband's life she must tell him not to leave her; if not it will be his death. Laine comes back for a moment to Marthe, but shows himself unable to effect his own salvation; therefore he will have to die, and soon after, indeed, while Thomas Pollock Nageoire's house blazes in the distance, a horse arrives carrying Laine's body. Léchy has killed him, and has also set the house on fire. The drama ends in an atmosphere of strange calm, with Marthe accepting her fate, and Thomas Pollock Nageoire having found, thanks to Marthe, his lost soul.

Claudel explained to his friend Marcel Schwob that the theme of *L'Échange* ' was a very personal one. I have,' he said, ' depicted myself under the guise of a young man who sells his wife in order to recover his freedom. Desire in all its aspects is expressed by the American actress, while the wife represents the sense of duty. I am all the main characters—the actress, the deserted wife, the wild young man, the business man. I have not aimed at any objective truth in the character of Léchy Elbernon, or in the judgment on her behaviour.' This straightforward confession explains and accounts for certain dramatic weaknesses of the play; at the same time it clearly shows Claudel's imaginative power to create strong resemblances with life. The plot is perhaps slightly mechanical; the characters tend to be types lacking the individuality which they should have in a drama; nevertheless they are well enough drawn to carry within them the seeds of their own destruction, and we have a plot and a tension which rise steadily until the *dénouement*.

L'Échange is a drama. Louis Laine and Léchy Elbernon have in them the violence of people who have not been tamed by centuries of organized social life and accepted moral principles. Their passions, their uncontrollable desires, urge them to ruin. Thomas Pollock Nageoire is a mixture of the old and the new worlds; under the thin film of ruthless business competition still lurks the old moral man of the ancient world, and in the end, thanks to Marthe, he rediscovers his soul. Marthe represents what is best in woman: firm faith in her principles, boundless human love, and trust in God's way. Her character rises to tragic pathos, her innocence is burdened with a fate which she does not deserve, she is acted upon by the violent passions of the other protagonists of the drama. She has upon her the marks of tragic grandeur, her suffering sounds real, and she can express her loneliness and plight in beautiful poetry, as in the very moving scene when Laine comes to tell her that he is leaving her, or when, at the beginning of the Third Act, she is alone on the sea-shore, away from her ancestral roots, without a friend near her. That monologue is certainly very good poetry, although it is perhaps rather long. Marthe, the chosen instrument of God's Will, belongs to the same family as Violaine and Dona Musique, the women born to heal wounds and to bring salvation to men, and her part contains the best poetry. There is also good poetry in the part of Léchy Elbernon, chiefly when, at the end of the Second Act, in front of Marthe, she asks Laine to follow her:

> Aime-moi, car je suis belle! Aime-moi, car je suis l'amour, et
> je suis sans règle et sans loi!
> Et je m'en vais de lieu en lieu, et je ne suis pas une seule femme,
> mais plusieurs, prestige, vivante dans une histoire inventée!
> Vis! sens en toi
> La puissante jeunesse qu'il ne sera pas aisé de contraindre.
> Sois libre! le désir hardi
> Vit en toi au-dessus de la loi comme un lion!
> Aime-moi, car je suis belle! et où s'ouvre la bouche, c'est là que
> j'appliquerai la mienne.
>
> (p. 696)

The theme of *L'Échange* is much like that of *Partage de Midi*. God's Will cannot be transgressed with impunity, and evil and all the suffering that it implies must be accepted in the belief that the ways of Providence, although inscrutable, lead men to the Supreme Good, and to happiness. We shall see with *Partage de Midi* the dramatic and theological implications of such beliefs. At this juncture one should note once more that the time has not yet come in Claudel's work when poetry and drama are absolutely one.

L'Échange illustrates very clearly, I think, the argument I have tried to elaborate in this study, an argument which aims at showing that what counts most in Claudel is the theme expounded by the story and the actions and the symbolical value of the characters, and their speeches. As Claudel himself has made clear, the characters are purely representations of conflicting aspects of his personality, and he involves them in actions and situations which will reveal to us and to himself what happens when certain forces of life are in conflict. The theme is the one which forms the crux of his experience; it is that God's ways are inscrutable, but that not until he accepts them can a man reach happiness ranging in intensity from earthly satisfaction to heavenly bliss within God's Will. The forces involved are two variations on the theme of sex—the sex impulse of destruction in Léchy, and sex restlessness in Laine— counterbalanced by the saintliness and faith of Marthe, with Thomas Pollock Nageoire as a necessary object upon which Divine Grace will operate through Marthe. The characters are symbols of those forces, and as is usually the case with Claudel, they tend towards the straight line, or the single colour, black, white, or red. They are not depicted in their subtle psychological complexities, with their hesitations, impulses, and changes, like the masterly creations of Racine; they are all of a piece, actuated by one single motive. which urges them on unswervingly. They are not, therefore, true to life; they are beyond life, they are expressions of life, they are life seen from a huge distance, from a point at which men's ways and passions merge into the few main streams which could be said to form the flow of mankind; or they are seen as the representations of the mysterious essences which underlie the actions of men. Therefore they are never fully explained, for they do not know themselves; they always stand in a half-light, termini of forces whose roots we cannot reach, and they move and act in un- avoidable ways as instruments of a purpose which is beyond man. Tête d'or goes to his end devoured by his self-centred ambition, the ambition which, when it is God-centred, as in the case of Rodrigue, can lead to heaven. Mara and Léchy hate and kill with the same steadfastness, the same singleness of purpose and faith in their actions which guide Marthe to forgiveness, and Violaine and Prouhèze to heaven. Ysé and Mésa accept their adulterous love with the full knowledge of their guilt, and yet with the hope that their love, part of God's Will, will be forgiven and they will be admitted to heaven. Claudel's characters live an elemental life; they are forces, black or white, which terrify us or fill us with admiration or pity; they are forces which we dimly recognize, with which we feel vague affinities, but which we could not analyse or imitate, for they are beyond life.

They are poetic representations of the conflicting aspects of man's nature, and as such partake of its mystery. Their life, although it takes place on the plane of reality, is based on a transcendentalism sometimes recognizable, acceptable, and part of human experience, sometimes unreal, and which makes their complete grasp impossible.

PARTAGE DE MIDI

FROM the very beginning of the play we realize that Ysé is an unpredictable woman, born for heroic deeds, a great force of nature, untied, harnessed to nothing, a boat riding at anchor, waiting for the wind. We cannot fail to wonder what is going to happen. Then we have Mésa, a man who is halfway between heaven and earth, a man who feels in himself a force which tries to lift him up, yet who is incapable of leaving the earth. There is in him the feeling of something unfulfilled, unfinished; the experience which will bring about his ripeness and fall has not taken place, yet one feels that this experience cannot be too far off. Ysé comes to him surrounded and preceded by a growing rumour of the extraordinary phenomenon which is going to tear off his roots and carry him away on its wings, to the only world where such lovers can live: to the world of Death. As soon as they meet they are both aware that they know each other, that the strands of their passion have been woven in the loom of Time, that they merely recognize each other and that, in spite of themselves, their human situation and their struggle, the hour has now come when they must accept the long-awaited experience which will transform them. ' *Mésa, je suis Ysé, c'est moi,*' says Ysé; and Mésa, who is still struggling to achieve peace with himself, aware of what Ysé really is for him, tries for a moment to avoid his fate, but he cannot. All has been willed. They are meant for each other like all the other extraordinary lovers of history, and their fate must be accepted.

From the beginning we realize that Mésa belongs to the small group of human beings who carry God in their hearts, and who, somehow, have not yet been touched by God's Grace. So they have still to be tested by great suffering, and they have to reach Him the hard way; they are like trees torn by hurricanes, wrapt in the agony of the fear that God might be lost forever.

Mésa also recognizes Ysé at once—*vous êtes Ysé, je sais que vous êtes Ysé*—and he recognizes in her the acme of his earthly desires and the measure of his doom, for she is the one whom he cannot have, and yet the one whom he wants, even if thereby he were to die for Eternity. We are here on the plane of tragedy. The two protagonists are placed face to face with a destiny which they cannot avoid; the forces which compel them forward are both internal and external, though they can be said to be external only in as far as their respective consciousnesses reveal to them what is, and what inevitably must be, irrespective of pain and disaster. Their situation is similar to that of Phèdre, with language used as the revelatory instrument of a hidden, unavoidable reality. Mésa needs God's Grace and is obviously not yet ready for it; for had he been ready, he might have resisted the sensuous love which throws him towards Ysé, and which is to destroy both. On the other hand, it is difficult to understand how a possible discrimination between physical and spiritual love can be God-made. The human creature is one, body and soul, and the only problem which arises is the problem of intention. Does Mésa love Ysé for herself or for himself? As Ysé points out to him, it looks as if for the moment he were preoccupied with himself: *Vous vous occupez de vous seul, il est plus facile, Mésa, de s'offrir que de se donner.*

The Second Act takes place in a cemetery in Hong Kong, and contains the decision and action which will bring about the catastrophe. It is possible to think that had De Ciz listened to his wife's entreaties, disaster might have been avoided; it seems to me that the scene between Ysé and De Ciz, which is dramatic, accentuates the weight of Mésa's guilt, and throws into relief Mésa's responsibility. It is Mésa who, between God and His creature, has chosen the creature; it is he who, before Ysé's arrival in the cemetery, had already decided and stood with:

> Mon âme en moi comme une pièce d'or entre les mains d'un joueur!

and at the end of the Act it is he who cunningly yet knowingly, like Pontius Pilate, sends De Ciz to his death. Mésa is in the hands of powers beyond his will; he has failed God, and he must, through Hell, return to God. The play still moves on the plane of tragedy, for the De Ciz–Ysé scene is there rather for poetic truth than for purely dramatic reasons.

In the Third Act we find that Ysé, after having lived for a year with Mésa, has left him to live with Amalric. She has had a child by Mésa, and at the beginning of the last Act we find Amalric, Ysé, and her child surrounded by Chinese rebels and sheltering in a wooden house which they have decided to blow up rather than allow themselves to be captured alive. While Amalric is absent for a moment, Mésa arrives unexpectedly, and in the course of a long soliloquy he reproaches Ysé with her desertion and silence. Ysé does not utter a word. Amalric returns, and after a brief fight Mésa is left broken-limbed on the floor. Ysé and Amalric search him and find a pass which will enable them to cross the Chinese lines and to reach safety. Mésa left alone prepares himself to make his peace with God, and to die. Unexpectedly Ysé returns and accepts death with him, with the shared hope that however arduous the road, however long the trial, they will meet again in Eternity.

The Third Act is extremely moving, though dramatically weak, and contains a shift from definite tragic pathos to the miracle play. We can understand the psychological reasons which broke the union of Ysé and Mésa. Mésa, who had been unable to give himself entirely to God, had also been unable to give himself entirely and definitely to Ysé. Ysé, who had broken her life, and tried to fill that terrible vacuum which only God could fill, had been unable to live for long in the extraordinary atmosphere which surrounded Mésa; therefore she had returned to Amalric, who is on a lower level, who is more human, and who has certain complementary assets which she needs. Her cynicism at the sight of Mésa's defeat at the hands of Amalric remains difficult to grasp psychologically, unless we admit a temporary loss of control, and that is not impossible in an hysterical character like that of Ysé. Her return to Mésa is psychologically consistent, and the only weakness of the play, if weakness there is, lies in the transition from the tragic pathos which surrounds both Ysé and Mésa up to the end, to the realization that all their sufferings endured, the deaths and disasters which have strewn the paths of their lives, were part of God's ways to bring back to Him souls which have strayed

[68]

from the flock, so that in the end Mésa can say, with faith in God:

Adieu! je t'ai vue pour la dernière fois!
Par quelles routes longues, pénibles,
Distants encore que ne cessant de peser
L'un sur l'autre, allons-nous
Mener nos âmes en travail?
Souviens-toi, souviens-toi du signe!
Et le mien, ce n'est pas de vains cheveux dans la tempête, et le
    petit mouchoir un moment,
Mais, tous voiles dissipés, moi-même, la forte flamme fulminante,
    le grand mâle dans la gloire de Dieu,
L'homme dans la splendeur de l'août, l'Esprit vainqueur dans la
    transfiguration de Midi!

(p. 989)

The dramatic weakness comes from the fact that we are here confronted with an experience which has not been truly imaginatively lived. This is the end which the poet wishes for these lovers, yet it is neither the end which he himself has been able to live through imaginatively, nor is it the end necessarily flowing from the preceding feelings of the characters involved. Ysé cannot be both Mésa's predestined lover and the instrument which through sin and suffering is going to bring him back to God; she cannot be both the jack-sin which through death is going to lift Mésa to heaven and the eternal reward which Mésa will enjoy in heaven—unless Claudel, by a kind of casuistry which few could accept, separates body and soul, presents Ysé's and Mésa's love as God's Will, and its consummation on earth as Satan's design. And even that would only be another aspect of the dichotomy which in Claudel's theology impinges seriously on the drama.

After his conversion, Claudel seems to have felt more and more as if he were a man endowed with one of God's voices, and therefore the quality of ' negative capability '—that quality of being able to remain in uncertainty and doubt, without any irritable reaching after facts and reasons, a quality which, as Keats pointed out, Shakespeare ' possessed enormously '—seems to have progressively disappeared from Claudel's artistic life. He ceased to be the poet who could say with Keats, ' When I

[69]

am in a room with people if ever I am free from speculating on creations of my own brain, then not myself goes home to myself, but the identity of every one in the room begins so to press upon me that I am in a very little time annihilated—not only among men; it would be the same in a nursery of children. . . .' In Claudel we have the prophet, the man of God, co-ordinating the poet's feeling from the outside and not allowing the feelings and sensations to co-ordinate themselves and to unfold with ever-renewed freshness, along the unbroken, ever-changing flow of consciousness which illumines and grows more and more powerful in order to reach out into the recesses of the unconscious mind. Claudel knew probably too well where he was going and what he was doing, and once he had his illumination on the road to Damascus he forgot too completely the doubts of St. Paul, those of St. Augustine, or the sensuous mysticism of St. John of the Cross, and his poetry suffered.

In *Partage de Midi* Claudel, though touched by the light of God's Grace, still retains some of the violence and pride of the Pagan. The play, which is very moving and one of the most lyrical plays ever written, owes a great deal of its pathos to the conflict between the beliefs and the uncertainties of the main protagonists, between the awareness of sin and the overwhelming desire to plunge into it, between the knowledge of God's love and God's Will, and the deadly urge to transgress them, carried away by the feeling that absolute possession of the being which belongs to God can be achieved only by death. Ysé knows her incompleteness, and she knows that, in spite of her passion or perhaps because of her passion, there exists an ineffable state, which human love, physical or spiritual, cannot create. Only in death can she reach that absolute, and so she consciously wills her death and that of her lover in an attempt to fulfil themselves in the face of God, they die in an apotheosis of pagan grandeur, yet they still trust in God's mercy, who will, they hope, sanction their love in Eternity.

The lyrical sweep of the verse matches the tense pathos of the emotions and makes the play one of the outstanding achievements of the theatre. The characters have, on the whole, lives of their own; we do not have the feeling of constant supernatural intervention. In spite of what Claudel says,

' that in order to take man away from himself, to enable him to have the knowledge of the other, there is only one appropriate instrument, woman ', in spite of the aspect of Claudelian dogmatism which states that God makes use of certain human beings as vessels of His Will, dogmatism is not too apparent in this play. It is true indeed that Mésa is a man who has had his revelation, without having become fit to be admitted into God's bosom, because he has retained his human pride and the arrogance of his purity without the awareness of sin, and this without God's Grace; therefore the woman is the instrument with which God will break him, will bring him to Himself through sin and humility. One can feel that, and one can feel also that if the central character of the play, Ysé, had been all of a piece, a single-minded instrument of Divine Providence, as Violaine for instance is, the play would have been mechanical. But Ysé is, up to the end, a real human being, unpredictable, uncontrollable, a force of nature, and a force which can manifest itself only through and by other beings, a force which becomes part of the pattern of life, which in the end she drags down with her into catastrophe.

But just as we shall see how Claudel transformed *La jeune fille Violaine*—a great poetic drama—into the mystery play called *L'Annonce faite à Marie*, in the same way we can see in *Partage de Midi* differences between the original and the final form which are not to the advantage of the latter. The new preface to the play, published in 1948, completely different from the original introduction, shows Claudel concerned with dogmatic preoccupations which seem to be posterior to the play, and should therefore not be taken too literally. Whether the Third Act has been slightly modified, in order to fit in with Claudel's theological view, I do not know, but the fact is that those preoccupations are too apparent there, and that the play would have been much greater without them. As it stands, the Third Act, which is beautiful poetry, is dramatically weak, for the solution that it offers is that of a morality play, and not that of a true drama. The ' cantique ' of Mésa is beautiful, but no longer quite in character, and above all Ysé, the vital character of the play, emerges, perhaps too clearly, as the chosen instrument of God; she has been the ' jack ' employed in order to

lift God's elect—Mesa—to Him. Such a view of the relationship between man and God fits Pagan deities perfectly, but it
does not fit the God of the Christians.

Whatever determinism one may believe in, whatever the force
and the extent of God's Will, we cannot accept the idea of a
God deliberately choosing certain victims for sacrifice, even in
order to see the accomplishment of His ways, which lead to the
supreme good. It is possible to believe in metaphysical
determinism and to accept the view that whatever is or exists
could not be or exist otherwise than as it does, but it seems to me
impossible to believe in God's choosing certain of His creatures to
scourge them in order to carry out His purpose. That is the
God of the Old Testament. The God of Claudel seems to me
too intent on ruling the lives of His creatures, punishing them, or
rewarding them. He never leaves them any respite. He is too
anthropomorphic; He is not the God of Love, and certain
aspects of His nature are rather repellent. Dramatic characters
can suffer from the obviously set purpose of their creator only
when they are too clearly there for a chosen end. Here it is
not the Greek's *ananke*, greater than the gods, and which
makes one pity the human suffering and the pathos of men and
women overwhelmed by superior forces. Here we have men
and women deliberately used to carry out God's Will, God's
conception of man's salvation. How can we pity Mésa, Ysé,
etc., if all that happened was entirely due to God's Will, for
their own good and for their eternal salvation? Who, if he
believes in God and eternity, will prefer his earthly joys to
eternal bliss, whatever human pains he has to go through in
order to reach it? In spite of his ardent Catholic apologists,
one has the feeling that it is Claudel's theology which is somehow wrong, for one cannot accept with equanimity the conception of a God who uses His creatures like puppets, a conception which seems to me remote from the doctrine of love and
forgiveness which brought the Redeemer to earth. The
vindication of the idea, *Le mal est dans le monde comme un esclave
qui fait monter l'eau* is difficult and well-nigh impossible to carry
out, and the attempt is harmful to the harmony of the play, for
as a result the *dénouement* is strained and lacks that character of
unavoidable necessity which could have made of it a truly

great play; the hand of the author is too obvious, and the heroes die in an apotheosis of fully explained morality and in full agreement with the Law. But this major flaw in Claudel's theology does not endanger *Partage de Midi* to the extent that it endangers *Le Soulier de Satin* or *L'Annonce faite à Marie*. In spite of the slightly strained didacticism of the last Act, in spite of the theological preoccupations of the Preface, which might well be described as one of Claudel's disastrous improvements, *Partage de Midi* is, with *La jeune fille Violaine*, second version, probably Claudel's greatest drama.

Claudel's anthropomorphism appears nowhere more clearly than in *Jeanne d'Arc au Bûcher;* in that play Joan of Arc, tied to the stake, talks to God and His angels for nearly two hours. Claudel does not seem to realize the impossibility of rendering God's voice and presence apprehensible to the human senses, nor the incongruity of such a convention in *Jeanne au Bûcher*, which seems to me a failure redeemed only by Honegger's music. Claudel's failure in regard to the apprehension of the Divinity is not a unique instance in literature; a greater poet than he—Milton—makes God speak through a human voice and brings the supernatural too close to the human plane. Dante was wiser than either, and in Canto XXX of *Il Paradiso* he tells us that he can give us only vague memories of his great mystical experience, which is beyond words. The whole convention of Joan of Arc tied to the stake and carrying on, amidst fire, a lengthy dialogue with God and His angels is unacceptable. Besides, the allegories have no freshness, no novelty, they are childish, unconvincing and lacking in sensitiveness; the play is, on the whole, merely bad rhetoric.

V

LA JEUNE FILLE VIOLAINE

La jeune fille Violaine, which became in the end *L'Annonce faite à Marie,* is probably Claudel's masterpiece, and possibly one of the great plays of the world. That play has taken fifty-six years to ripen and to reach its final form, and it has gone through four consecutive versions, including two different readings for the last Act. What the play means to the author, what pains he has taken to try to give us a work of art, Claudel himself tells us in an interview with *Le Monde,* 9th March, 1948. '*L'Annonce faite à Marie* is the fruit of fifty-six years of arduous and patient work; this play deals with some of my most personal feelings, its message is the kind of exultation which faith imparts to the most natural forces of men. In the last version I have increased the importance of Mara's part. She believes that God can do her good, and that conviction arises from her naturally egotistic instincts. She compels God to resurrect her dead daughter through Violaine who, by her sacrifice, becomes the instrument of the miracle. "The kingdom of God suffers violence", that phrase from the Bible could be used as an exergue to my play.' Claudel's intentions are here made clear, and we see how, in spite of Mara's wickedness and criminal egoism, the Kingdom of God suffers violence and satisfies her faith in miracles. For, although Violaine says that the reborn child was the only living token of her love for Jacques Hury, the miracle also satisfies Mara's passionate desire to keep alive that only fruit of her ill-gotten love, and in the end she says:

> Pourquoi Dieu ne reste-t-il pas chez lui et vient-il nous déranger?
> notre malheureuse vie est si courte! qu'il nous y laisse du
> moins en paix!
>
> (p. 641, vol. I)

This is no expression of love for a God whose existence is nevertheless not denied. In as far as Claudel's explanation goes, the

play surely means that God accepts evil as perhaps a necessary
part of the greater good, that His ways are beyond the comprehension of the human creature, and His forgiveness is infinite.
But there is obviously more to it than that: there is the problem
here implied that if evil is part of the greater good, then God is
responsible for both; Mara is as much the instrument of His
will as Violaine, and she is part of the miracle which creates
Violaine's sainthood, in the same way as Lucifer, the fallen
angel, is a necessary part of the Redemption, for on the metaphysical plane there is no hazard, there is only God's Will, and
also God's grace to those who hope and pray.

In another interview published in the *Figaro Littéraire*, 11th
March, 1948, Claudel said: ' I am eighty years old and this is
the crowning stone of my dramatic and poetic work '.   I do not
know whether or not we should take him literally, but such a
statement confirms once more the great importance that Claudel
attached to that play.   Here we have indeed characters
drawn with a masterly stroke, dramatic tension sustained to the
end, and magnificent poetry.   Yet I cannot help feeling that,
in spite of Claudel's patient efforts, the result is not quite satis-
factory.   I am aware that this may sound like heresy to certain
ears, and also that mine is very much a solitary voice, but my
feeling is that *La jeune fille Violaine*, second version is a much
greater play than *L'Annonce faite à Marie*, its final form; it is
possibly a great play, and certainly one of Claudel's major
achievements.   *L'Annonce faite à Marie* is too much a mystery-
play-cum-historical pageant.   The symbolism, the intentions
of the author, and his theological views, are too prominent, and
they hamper its dramatic development.   Some characters
which in *La jeune fille Violaine* were not too clearly outlined and
had a powerful poetic ambiguity, have here been humanized;
others which, on the contrary, were very human, like Anne
Vercors, have drawn near to the symbol; all of them seem to
have been attuned by the process, on a key which clarifies the
intentions of the author, but which is definitely at a lower
pitch.   An analysis of the three plays, *La jeune fille Violaine*, first
and second versions, and *L'Annonce faite à Marie*, will show the
line followed by Claudel, and the definite transformation which
has taken place.

F

La jeune fille Violaine—First Version

The action takes place at Combernon, a big farm in Champagne.

Act I. Anne Vercors explains how his wife, Elizabeth, has, after seven years, given him two daughters, Violaine and Bibiane. Anne Vercors, an old peasant at the end of his days, wants to leave his land to go away, he does not know where, towards the sea (like Rimbaud or Simon Agnel). He wants to leave somebody in charge of his family and his lands; he decides to marry Violaine to Jacquin Uri. Violaine loves Jacquin who loves her, but Bibiane also loves Jacquin and she will do anything rather than give him up.

Act II. Bibiane has confided her feelings to her mother, who has told Violaine. Violaine decides to sacrifice herself and to turn down Jacquin Uri so that he may marry her sister. In the scene in the garden Jacquin thinks that she refuses to marry him because she is in love with Eloi Baube, Violaine's cousin, who has just left to marry Lidine. When Jacquin accuses Violaine, she lets him believe that she has been seduced. Violaine accepts the insult in the eyes of all those who are dearest to her—her former fiancé, her mother and her sister. She begins to walk the path of the saint. She divests herself of her riches in favour of her sister, and she leaves the house cursed by Bibiane and in a state of great distress; she soon becomes blind.

In the *Third Act* Baube meets Violaine in the woods; he tells her that he does not love his wife, and that he is not happy with her. Violaine tells him what he ought to do, and he goes away having been given plenty to think about. Bibiane arrives with her blind son Aubin, and asks Violaine to cure his blindness. All sorts of people—beggars and an old woman who hopes to be cured—are around them. Violaine restores little Aubin's sight.

Act IV. Bibiane has savagely assaulted Violaine. Violaine is brought back to die in Jacquin Uri's house; she tells him the truth about what happened; she is dying. Anne Vercors, her father, returns. He accepts everything as perfectly natural, he does not show any feelings of distress, he can think only of his voyage, and he talks about Rome; he gives us a description of his visit and an eulogy of the Pope which have nothing much to do with the play; his conversation with the Pope is a transposition to a kind of epic plane which does not suit either the situation or the narrator—the peasant—and makes it sound grotesque. The eulogy of Rome and the Pope may have pleased Claudel, but is completely irrelevant to the play.

In the end *La jeune fille Violaine* is neither drama nor tragedy, it is rather a haphazard construction which partakes of both, but which is above all an unsatisfactory attempt to transpose certain concepts, ideas, and feelings of Claudel on to the plane of realities. There is no plot, and there is no kind of compulsion, external or internal, which weighs over the characters and could produce pathos. Anne Vercors' departure from his house is a completely arbitrary and irresponsible gesture. There is a certain amount of pathos in Violaine's character, but on the whole the play is half-way between the mystery play and a combination of drama and tragedy and is wholly unsatisfactory.

La jeune fille Violaine—Second Version

Act I. Pierre de Craon meets Violaine for the last time. The scene sets the atmosphere of the play; we are on the human plane, on the plane where two beings recognize the great affinities which link them together, and also on the supra-human plane where those same two beings are dimly aware that there are in them forces which will tear them away from their roots towards the world of Light and Supreme Goodness. That First Scene maintains its moving ambiguity in beautiful poetry —Anne Vercors announces that he must go to America to help the family of his brother, who has just died (that decision has dramatic interest and psychological truth). Mara declares that if Violaine marries Jacques Hury she will kill herself. Anne Vercors leaves his home.

Act II. The mother tells Mara that she has spoken to Violaine about what she, Mara, intends to do if the marriage takes place. Jacques Hury arrives to see Violaine; Mara tells him that Violaine is really in love with Pierre de Craon. She tells him what she has seen. The dramatic tension increases. The scene between Violaine and Jacques is both dramatic and pathetic; Violaine accepts sorrows which she has not deserved. Violaine sets off on her road to Calvary, she has understood her destiny. Violaine signs away her heritage, and Mara throws ashes in her face. This is a very moving scene full of pathos.

Act III. The scene between Mara and Violaine is also both moving and very pathetic; here we have the extraordinary poetry of Violaine's revelation of God's force in her. *Je crois que tu peux me faire du bien,* says Mara, and so Violaine decides to act. The scene is also dramatic because of the progress of the action; Violaine gives another proof of her saintliness, and in so doing we have one more proof of God's mysterious will.

Act IV. Mara has murdered Violaine. This time Pierre de Craon comes back carrying Violaine in his arms. Here again we have an extremely moving scene, beautiful, and full of pathos. The return of Anne Vercors, with his unnatural detachment about Violaine's death and his slighting remarks about the Americans, introduces the only jarring note in an otherwise most moving Act, which continues with the pathos of Jacques Hury's suffering, the tragic force of Mara's hatred, which is as ineluctable as Fate and acts like poison in the blood, and ends with the magnificent dialogue between Pierre de Craon and Anne Vercors.

This is tragedy, Christian tragedy—perhaps one of the most moving of Christian tragedies. The forces which shape the destinies of the characters remain mysterious enough, and therefore leave the pathos of the extraordinary situations completely untouched. We are aware that a great power casts its shadow over the play and that Violaine, Pierre de Craon, and Anne Vercors—and in fact all the characters—are part of a pattern shaped by a supra-human Will. But in this tragedy, in which human beings write in blood the pattern of God's Will on earth, the characters retain their complex and moving humanity, and although some of them walk the way of the saint, they do it with painful, halting steps and with feelings which give rise to the most moving pathos. Although at the end of the play we might be tempted to say that all is well as it happened, and that it could only happen that way, this is the kind of conclusion which we might reach by ourselves, but which has not been foisted upon us in the course of the play by the obviously moralizing intentions of the author. We feel that we have witnessed part of the life of characters endowed with a poignant humanity expressed in moving and beautiful poetry.

L'Annonce faite à Marie

Prologue. Violaine is marked as God's creature from the beginning. Pierre de Craon, who has dared to touch her, is struck with leprosy. Then follows Pierre de Craon's earthly vision—the Queen-Mother's coming to Monsanvierge—and he must open the walls of the monastery for her passage. From the beginning we are on a plane different from that of *La jeune fille Violaine*—the plane of pageantry-cum-mystery-play. At once we are made aware that the love of Pierre de Craon for Violaine is more human than it was in *La jeune fille Violaine*, second version.

Act I. Anne Vercors wants to go to Jerusalem. France is divided, Christianity is divided; he wants to go in the name of his Dead, and he gives us a long account of his ancestry, tracing himself back to St. Rémy of Rheims.

Act II opens with Mara and her mother, later Mara and Jacques Hury are together. Then follows a scene which brings together Jacques and Violaine; Violaine in her conventional Monsanvierge dress introduces a ritualistic atmosphere, she draws towards the symbol, and lowers the human element of the scene. She tells Jacques that she has leprosy; he baulks, and refuses to marry her, and she decides to go and join the special camp for those who have her disease. 'Take your travelling clothes,' says Jacques, and she goes away. The fact that Violaine no longer endures silently Jacques' insults and tormenting questions, but, on the contrary, throws the onus of the decision on him by telling him that she has leprosy, the lowering of the human element in order to draw nearer to the symbolism and ritualism of the Church takes away the pathos of the scene. Even more, since Jacques is not prepared to accept Violaine with her disease, he is considerably diminished in stature, and appears as a man of little courage and shallow love.

Act III. Mara goes to see Violaine, and we have the miracle. This time the child is dead; Violaine has to bring him back to life, and so she does, on Christmas night. The bells are ringing in the distance announcing the passage of the King and Joan of Arc towards Rheims. Mara reads extracts from the Bible. Then at that moment when the bells are ringing again to celebrate the anniversary of the birth of Christ, Aubaine, Mara's daughter, is resurrected.

Act IV. Anne Vercors returns carrying the body of Violaine, which he has found in a ditch, and he tells Jacques Hury that everything that has been, has been for the greater good. Joan of Arc has died for France, the Pope is back in Rome, Pierre de Craon is cured, and Violaine did what she did because she had heard God's voice, and like him she had to leave behind all earthly things. Anne Vercors excuses Mara for having done what she has done because she was not responsible, and Violaine dies amidst a general reconciliation and in an atmosphere of holiness. In the last Act of *L'Annonce faite à Marie* the meeting between Violaine and Jacques is less moving than in *La jeune fille Violaine*, second version. In the stage version, in the one in which Pierre de Craon does not appear, it is less moving still because the protagonists are far more dehumanized, and they have already left the earth for heaven.

To me a great deal of the extraordinary beauty of the beginning of the First Act of *La jeune fille Violaine* is lost in *L'Annonce faite à Marie*. The ambiguity of Pierre de Craon's character and of his love has disappeared. In *L'Annonce faite à Marie* he is an architect, talking of his building plans, a man who knows his calling and who can feel it in those who, like him, have heard that calling, but he is also a disappointed lover who must do a great deal of apologizing and explaining away of his behaviour; he has to confess that he hates his rival, and instead of the splendid cosmic poetry of *La jeune fille Violaine* beginning with

> L'eau m'a séduit.
> Tout ce qui vit, depuis la plante jusqu'à l'homme,
> Intérieurement par l'eau; et c'est pourquoi, le coeur altéré
> De la connaissance de ce qui vit, dès l'enfance,
> J'ai attaché mon coeur et mon esprit sur l'eau vive et vivifiante;
> L'eau subtile et liquide, circulante, ambiante, médiatrice, source
> première et veine commune.

(p. 576)

[80]

and continuing right to the end of the scene, we have the lover's passionate speech which is human and moving, but which lowers the level of the poetry, and of the play, whose purpose, being now evident, takes the form of a demonstration. Pierre de Craon is certainly much greater in his silence, in his ambiguous love and in his heartrending awareness that there is in him a thirst which cannot be quenched than in his more clear-cut character in *L'Annonce faite à Marie*. In the same way Violaine, when she has not been tried and pursued by Pierre de Craon, whom she wounds in self-defence, has a much greater elemental power than in *L'Annonce faite à Marie*, and she is much greater when she meets Jacques and remains silent, than when she goes to him elegantly attired and alluring, in spite of all the symbolism and ritualism of the dress. She shows in that latter scene some traces of the coquetry which had already been noticeable in the previous scene with Pierre de Craon; and the rather conventional pattern of the beginning, followed by certain martial strains which apply to God as well as to man, and the melodramatic display of the mark of leprosy at the end, have none of the pathos which pervaded the same scene in *La jeune fille Violaine*. The idea of sending Anne Vercors to Jerusalem and not to America for family reasons, fits in the atmosphere of the mystery-play, diminishes the suggestive power of the play, and lowers its emotional tension because the reasons for Vercors' departure are not plausible enough, not even on the plane of faith and divine grace:

Je suis las d'être heureux

are ill-fitting words in the mouth of a man of God, and they tend to suggest the character of a rather irresponsible and restless old man. His duty, his supreme duty, which is the fulfilment of God's Will, is to do his allotted task on earth. His decision to leave his family is completely arbitrary, and leads him out of the Christian pattern of life as outlined by Pierre de Craon; in that pattern every man must perform his task, however humble and wearisome it may be, and not down tools and set off for Jerusalem and the golden East, or for any other earthly magic spot. Anne Vercors says that he has heard the call of the Trumpet and that he is going to the Holy Land as the

[81]

representative of all his dead, in order to pray for the forlorn, divided kingdom of France. But surely that all-too-simple excuse cannot be accepted. He puts on a garb which is obviously not made for him. His dead could bring him back to Adam, and the presumptuousness of this peasant of Champagne is completely out of place, in spite of the fact that Joan of Arc was born not far away from the spot where he lives, and that her name is often mentioned there. In her case her life and her achievements are the test of her saintliness, but to go to the Holy Land has nothing much to do with sainthood, and this decision is out of character.

The beautiful poetry of Anne Vercors, talking about the earth in *La jeune fille Violaine,* is missing here, and we have instead an historical exposition of the past of the Vercors and their lands, a thorough search for a pedigree, a search which, in the mouth of this peasant, does not ring true, and only serves to show Claudel's preoccupations, which are didactic and sentimental, but not dramatic. In fact, the stress on the pageantry aspects of the mystery-play, all those historical references to Joan of Arc, to the King of France coming to Rheims, to the mysterious association between the monastery of Monsanvierge and the Vercors, and all the pomp and ceremonial of names in order to accentuate the symbolism of the play only succeed in stressing its allegorical, abstract, and unreal aspect, and diminish its dramatic quality. The attempt to provide Violaine with a noble pedigree is made in order to bring closer the analogy between her and the Virgin Mary, but it only succeeds in straining the symbolism of the play, which is too near an analogy of the great Birth. An analogy is after all only an analogy. The symbolism of the leprosy, the scourge of God to punish Pierre de Craon's failing, the leprosy of Violaine freely accepted and reminiscent of Christ's freely accepted suffering, the symbolism of the birth which takes place on Christmas night amidst hymns, readings from the Bible and the whole traditional background of the great night—ringing bells, distant trumpets announcing the passage of the King towards Rheims, Joan of Arc and voices of angels—all that is too forced. In the previous version Violaine was only restoring sight to the blind child; in *L'Annonce faite à Marie* she has to restore life to the dead child. The principle of the miracle is the same in both cases, and therefore it cannot be called into question, but here the change is made in order to bring Violaine nearer the person of the Blessed Virgin. The predestination which weighs on Violaine born in Monsanvierge is too strongly stressed; we have a repetition of the great Birth without the poignancy and the powerful meaning of the original; in the end the whole theme has lost a considerable amount of its dramatic and, above all, its tragic force.

I am well aware that these reservations are, for the moment, without support from other critics; I am also dimly aware that I may be over-sensitive to the obviousness and forcefulness of Claudel's theology in his drama; on the other hand, I feel convinced of the validity of the remarks I have made about *L'Annonce faite à Marie* as a poetic drama. A great deal of the splendid poetry of *La jeune fille Violaine* is also found in *L'Annonce faite à Marie,* but the atmosphere being slightly different, the dramatic tension being lower, the poetic power of the words does not rise and sing with the same exalting and moving force. I said the dramatic tension, for it is possible that for souls devotedly attuned to that of Claudel's the mystery-play is far more moving than the drama, and the poetry is there; it is a matter of degree, and the only reason why I quote from *La jeune fille Violaine* is that, in my view, the poetic level is, on the whole, higher than that of *L'Annonce faite à Marie.*

The tone is set by the first scene, which is a magnificent prelude, foretelling the whole drama, and rising to heights unsurpassed in the course of the play; then we have the metaphor of the water, with its deep meaning and symbolism:

Comment me ferais-je comprendre, comparant la mort avec la vie?
L'amour que vous allez connaître est semblable à l'humiliation de la mort, à la résolution de la dernière heure,
Et un homme nouveau naît de ce consentement réciproque, du double et funèbre aveu.
Mais l'autre amour se tient à toutes ces portes par lesquelles nous recevons la vie,
La bouche qui goûte et qui boit, les narines qui aspirent, les oreilles et les yeux qui écoutent et qui considèrent.

[83]

Et l'intelligence qui apprend, qui comprend et qui conçoit;
Et toutes ensemble s'ouvrent dans ce mouvement par lequel
    notre poitrine se soulève.
Et tel est le principe, le mouvement primitif et profond de
    l'être que je constitue.
L'acte même par lequel je suis.
Et cette soif comporte pour qu'elle existe la source; l'Insatiable
    ne peut
S'appliquer que sur l'Inépuisable.

(p. 579)

We understand at once that here we have two beings who are
not on the normal level of life, and, carried away by their words
to realms beyond man, and yet where man lives, we feel that
this is truly great poetry. The dramatic significance of Pierre
de Craon's gesture, testing with his nail the solidity of the wall,
as he had just tested the spiritual solidity of Violaine's faith,
cannot escape notice—it is a gesture which shows Claudel's
mastery in that remarkable scene. And this is not a lonely
flight into regions which afterwards fade away from our sight;
Claudel reaches those heights more than once. Following the
moving simplicity, the compressed violence of the poetry in the
scene between Jacques and Violaine, and the two very moving
scenes between Violaine and Mara, the one before Violaine
leaves the house, the second when she is blind and lives alone in
a cave, we have Violaine's revelation of her awareness of God's
presence, which is penetrating, extremely moving poetry, and
which surely has the signs of greatness:

Tout arrive par la secrète volonté de Dieu. Il est des fruits qui
    mûrissent à leur aise
Du printemps jusqu'à l'automne dans le soleil clément.
Et d'autres comme la grappe de raisin
Dont l'on tord la queue pour qu'elle soit noire plus tôt
Et qu'elle soit mise dans la main de la Vierge au jour de la
    Bonne-Dame.
Mara, tu as coupé le lien qui me tenait, et je ne repose plus que
    dans la main de Dieu même
—Et qui connaîtra le mieux un homme, celui qui de temps en
    temps
Lui rend visite par honnêteté ou par intérêt, ou la servante
Qui attend son pain de son maître?

[84]

Celle-là le sait par coeur.
Non point seulement dans son extérieur,
Mais dans ses secrètes habitudes domestiques.

(p. 616)

And following Mara's retort:

Je n'entends point cela. Dieu est à l'église et nous ne ferons
     point notre maison de la sienne. Il faut vivre avec ses
     pareils,

(p. 617)

we have Violaine's sublime reply, which shows how, rejected by
man, she felt God in her, and which is great poetry perfectly in
character and beyond character. It should be quoted in full;
but at least here is the end:

Et je m'attendais à une réponse, mais je reçus dans mon âme et
     dans mon corps
Plus qu'une réponse, le tirement de toute ma substance,
Comme le secret enfermé au coeur des planètes, le rapport
     propre
De mon être à un être plus grand.
C'est ainsi que, comme les astres les chemins de la nuit, tout
     brillants d'une lumière qu'ils ignorent,
Il me mène parmi les hommes, aveugle et close.

(p. 619)

The scene continues on that high level, tense with emotion,
stirring up personal problems like that of faith and Divine
Grace:

Qui mange le fruit, il faut qu'il l'aime, et avant d'y mordre,
     l'ayant reconnu, qu'il le cueille.
Mais que nul ne le tâte de ses mains curieuses, car les lèvres
     tendres et confiantes, seule la bouche obscure
Le peut recevoir; la chair
Aveugle et savoureuse, l'enveloppe de nuit
Ne peut fondre que dans la bouche seule, afin que le coeur
     accueille le germe bienfaisant.
Et ainsi ce fruit échappe à ceux qui le cherchent avec les mains
Et non point avec leur coeur, et non point pour son goût, mais
     pour son utilité.

(p. 622)

This is followed by Mara's joy at the sight of her child's restored sight.

Then we have the end, the last Act, the death of Violaine, her father's return home and the Biblical diatribe of Mara, who seems to embody the spirit of evil, symbolizing in her struggle and crime the two aspects of life—the good and the bad, Abel and Cain:

> Pourquoi Dieu ne reste-t-il pas chez lui et vient-il nous déranger? notre malheureuse vie est si courte! qu'il nous y laisse du moins en paix!
>
> (p. 641)

And the play ends with the serene duo of Anne Vercors and Pierre de Craon, with the calm acceptance of all—suffering and death—as being part of God's Will. Here we have the final song of two men, both intent, each one in his own way, on following God. These are the words of Anne Vercors:

> Pierre de Craon, nos pensées ne sont point les mêmes.
> Comme la lyre des anciens poètes, je sais
> Qu'il est des hommes que la bosse entre leurs deux paumes d'un bloc de terre
> Enivre comme une main mystérieuse saisie et comme une voix gémissante.
> De même pour vous, sculpteur nouveau, vous sentez dans vos doigts
> Le tas humain comme une glaise vivante.
> Et, tout plein du bouillonnement de l'esprit, vous voudriez lui donner la figure de votre amour.
> Mais moi, je suis pareil aux boeufs qui labourent les champs de la terre, d'un pas égal à celui des constellations.
> Ma vie a été réglée par les astres, j'ai fait ma tâche comme le soleil.
>
> (p. 652)

Here we have both the human effort towards God and the more profound spiritual effort to serve God in poetry whose moving beauty is worthy of the best that men have ever achieved.

VI

LE SOULIER DE SATIN

THE stage version of the play is divided into two parts and an epilogue; the parts are sub-divided into days.

Part One

First Day: Overture and Scene One. The announcer opens the play and tries to make contact with the audience by taking them into his confidence and telling them what is going to happen. He is followed by the Jesuit Father, who states the theme of the play in a prayer which contains a great deal of Claudel's theology. One cannot fail to note here two things of importance: the first one is that the symbolism of the Jesuit Father tied to the mast is strongly reminiscent of Christ nailed to the Cross, the second is the attempt to produce a cosmic drama by choosing to have the whole of the planet as the stage of an action which transcends time.

The second scene which follows introduces to us Don Pélage and Don Balthazar. It enables us to realize at once that Don Pélage is an upright and truthful man who has full confidence in the loyalty of his wife—Dona Prouhèze.

The scene which brings together Camille and Prouhèze is very important, in that it develops certain of the implications of the theme stated by the Jesuit Father. As soon as we meet Dona Prouhèze we are made aware of the fact that she is not truly in love with her husband, and that on the day that she meets somebody whom she will love, she will give up everything for him, even her life if needs be; we realize that we have before us an extraordinary woman, born to accomplish great things and to carry out God's purpose as outlined by the Jesuit Father. Camille strikes us as the condottieri type and also as a man who has in his heart a void waiting to be filled; he is in a state of instability and despair or '*Angst*', ready for the faith which could redeem and save him, and we cannot but feel

[87]

that Prouhèze's nature is such that if she realizes that it is God's Will that she should save him, she has in her the strength to do so, whatever moral suffering she may have to endure. Camille, however heathen he may be, has enough awareness of God's presence to know that the only way to tempt Prouhèze is not by her weaknesses, which do not exist, but by her strength.

The fifth scene continues the exposition. Here we have confirmation of what we had already guessed: that Dona Prouhèze is a woman of character, that she is desperately in love with a young man called Rodrigue, to whom she would surrender body and soul if she could, and that she is going to use every means at her disposal to try to rejoin him. But here is the problem: she cannot forget her duty to Don Pélage and the sacred laws of marriage. She is therefore faced with irreconcilable conditions: her awareness of having been made by God to love Rodrigue, and the realization that somehow, something has gone wrong in the strong links of the chain of predestination, for although she was meant for Rodrigue, she has married Don Pélage within God's laws. What is she going to do? What is going to happen? Here is the problem of the play, a problem which does not seem to offer any possibility of reconciling two contradictory things, both God-willed. A hint of a possible solution is contained in the fact that Dona Prouhèze declares her absolute love for Rodrigue and informs her guardian, Don Balthazar, of her plans, and above all she asks the Holy Virgin, Mother of All, source of Divine Grace, to protect her and to prevent her from doing something which in the end she seems to consider as a failing, in spite of her belief that her love for Rodrigue is God-willed. This kind of theology obviously strikes at the very roots of dramatic development, for from the beginning we know that everything is in God's hands through His ministering angels, and we know that in the end Prouhèze and Rodrigue cannot, and will not fail. Consequently we cannot have any dramatic suspense, at least nothing intense and embracing the whole movement of the play. The events which take place are neither parts of the development of character, nor the means of showing us characters in action; they are above all the changing tableaux which illustrate God's multifarious and mysterious ways and singleness of purpose. The fate of the *dénouement* is never in the balance; we neither apprehend it nor half-expect it, we know it, for it is stated at the beginning that God's purpose is not meant to be, and cannot be, thwarted.

If we cannot view the play as drama, can we view it as a tragedy resting wholly on the pathos born from the suffering of the heroes? One cannot but feel strong doubts about the latter view, for although there is undeserved suffering, that suffering is neither caused by blind ruthless fate, nor by capricious gods using human beings as the pawns in their celestial games; this suffering is, on the contrary, God-meant; and, if so, can we blame Him for it? Some of us perhaps might, but for all those who see in it a mighty justification of His ways to man, the play is, and can only be, a miracle-play.

Scene Six brings out just one aspect of Rodrigue's character, but a very interesting aspect—his independence; we realize that he is a man. Scene Seven confirms our first impression as to the nature of the play and strengthens the view that the author has made no attempt at verisimilitude or at presenting us with a logical development of characters and events and with scenes following one another in a plausible way. We have a mere succession of tableaux, and the main characters walk in and out of them at the discretion of the author, who seems to handle them as parts of a vast puppet show. The actions and movements of the characters are related to one another and integrated by the seeing eye and the controlling hand of the author. It is a process which is very much exploited by modern novelists, from Dos Passos to Sartre. In this tableau we catch a glimpse of all the characters of the play; Rodrigue and his Chinese servant occupy the foreground, and the important point here is Rodrigue's conversation with his confidant. That conversation is a strengthening of the theme stated at the beginning by the Jesuit Father, who might be regarded as the bass of the trio; then the theme, after having been taken up and expanded with some feminine touches by Prouhèze (soprano), is stated clearly in its final form by Rodrigue (tenor). He loves Prouhèze, but he knows that their union is impossible in this world:

Et crois-tu donc que ce soit son corps seul qui soit capable
    d'allumer dans le mien un tel désir?
Ce que j'aime,
Ce n'est point ce qu'il y a en elle de trouble et de mêlé et
    d'incertain que je lui demande, ce qu'il y a d'inerte et de
    neutre et de périssable,
C'est ce qui est la cause d'elle-même,
C'est l'être tout nu, la vie pure,
C'est cet amour aussi fort que moi sous mon désir comme une
    grande flamme crue, comme un rire dans ma face!
Ce n'est point son corps chéri jamais qui réussirait à me
    contenter!

(p. 886)

Prouhèze makes a brief appearance on the stage, then disappears, and she and Rodrigue are spared qualms of conscience
and possible troubles by the author, who very opportunely
produces an attack by brigands against pilgrims and the
Venerable Statue of St. James, which they are carrying; of
course Rodrigue, the true knight errant, has to leave his
private affairs and fly to the rescue of the Statue and the
Faith. This action is symbolical of the whole of his life, and
throughout he will always place his duty to God and man before
the longings of his heart. The sergeant and the negress seem
to be part of a fantasy by Walt Disney; this effect is clearly
brought out by the sergeant's words to the negress when he tells
her that, as in all fairy-stories, there is always a messenger, a
sergeant or Mercury who is ready to do whatever is required
to bring Prince and Princess together. This incident certainly
strengthens the puppet-like aspect of the play.

Scene Nine is a duet on the theme of love, with Dona
Prouhèze and Dona Musique. To Dona Musique love is joy,
for Prouhèze love is the absolute, the whole being, but with no
possible complete possession on earth. So for Rodrigue she
will be:

Une Épée au travers de son coeur.

Scenes Ten and Eleven increase the pantomime aspect of the
play. On one side we have Rodrigue's fight to rescue Don
Fernand and Dona Isobel, a fight in the course of which
Rodrigue is wounded, on the other we have the negress dancing

naked in the moonlight, her clothes standing stiff by her side, a big fish gazing at her and at her performance, which is interrupted by the unexpected arrival of Rodrigue's Chinese servant. This scene, meant perhaps for comic relief, is altogether incongruous and is a good example of Claudel's mixture of genres; the quick succession of tableaux produces a strong cinematic effect.

Scene Twelve, the scene between Prouhèze and her guardian angel, seems to me completely unconvincing. That mixture of reality and allegory is difficult to accept. In spite of the vast symbolism of the background and its connotations with the Bible, the angel has more in common with a stern schoolmaster than with an angel. The action is here held up by fantastic devices which belong to miracle and mystery-plays; the scene which follows, with Don Balthazar and L'Alfarès, offers no progress in the action or in the development of characters.

Scene Fourteen, the siege scene, is a tragi-comic scene. Don Balthazar's special brand of humour is difficult to grasp; his gargantuan meal, his playing about with the Chinese, his refusal to accept a truce while he sees that Dona Musique, the cause of the affray, has already disappeared, is worthy of an *opéra-bouffe*, but not of a serious play, and does not provide comic relief, if such were intended by the author.

Second Day: Scene One. The announcer is obviously meant to act as a chorus, knowing all, controlling all; in fact he strikes us as being, more than anything else, a circus-master. His supercilious attitude, his thundering voice, his bustling activity produce a comic effect; but is that effect wanted? In reality he is used as a means to hold together scenes and events which are too heterogeneous, too remote, to fit normally within the organic texture of the play; unfortunately the obviousness of the device is such as to jar on one's nerves, and it tends to impair our sympathy for and belief in the feelings of the other characters.

The next scene, between Dona Honoria and Don Pélage, is very moving, the action progresses and new facets of the characters' psychology come to light. First we learn something about Don Pélage himself, then about his relationship with Dona Prouhèze, and also about certain traits of her character. Don Pélage appears as the man with a rigid sense of discipline, set on the letter of the law, sometimes to the neglect of its spirit. He knows where the truth lies, he knows what a higher authority would say to him, yet he chooses to be the judge, the one who cannot forgive. Christ's spark of love is completely absent from his character. He knows how to tempt Prouhèze by her virtues, he knows what arguments to use with her. By so doing he compels us to realize that under the cloak of ' the law ' he is most ' unjust ', and he loses our sympathy.

Scene Three, with Dona Prouhèze and her husband, is one of the central scenes of the play. Don Pélage takes advantage of Prouhèze's strong sense of duty; he knows that she will never refuse to undertake a desperate task if she feels that it is her duty to do so and if she feels that she is the only one who could attempt it. To her plea that a love as pure as hers could not be evil, Don Pélage can only reply that what does not do any good is bad—a statement which means nothing. Yet he succeeds in persuading her to avoid Rodrigue for Rodrigue's sake and to go and face up to her duty in Africa.

Scene Five, between the King of Spain and Don Pélage, brings out clearly the fact that both Prouhèze and Rodrigue are tragic figures born to accomplish great things and to stand as examples to the rest of mankind. They are to be swept by powerful passions, to rise to great heights, to die miserably amidst the ingratitude and the neglect of those who have benefited from their efforts; they must be able to overcome all temptations and to accept any form of sacrifice. Rodrigue and Prouhèze must be able to meet, to know that they love each other desperately, and yet they must be able to part and to devote themselves to the accomplishment of their respective tasks on earth.

Scene Six, between Rodrigue and the captain of his boat, tends to show one really human aspect of Rodrigue's character. Like all lovers, he endures with difficulty what he supposes to be the pangs of unrequited love, and he is angry at the thought of having been deserted for Camille. He swears he will get hold of Prouhèze and compel her to submit to his will. With such thoughts in his mind, he is obviously straying from the

path towards Heaven which has been laid for him; at that
timely moment, therefore, the wreckage of the ' Santiago ',
the ship in which his Jesuit Brother was drowned, appears
again on the waves as a warning that he must remember and
follow God's ways. The wreckage knocks three times against
his boat, then disappears for good. Even the symbolism of
numbers is rigorously maintained.

Scene Seven shows that Prouhèze is in complete control of
the situation and is not afraid of being alone with Camille.
Scene Eight, which follows, begins like a comic opera, with
pasteboard settings, idyllic music, and the announcer doing a
lot of miming. We have a Romeo and Juliet operatic duet
in a scene which has no intrinsic beauty and which does not
contribute anything to the action; it is merely an operatic
interlude with samples of colloquial language (*boustife la
boustifaille*) thrown in in order to produce an air of youthful
freshness and unconventionality.

Scene Nine, with Don Camille and Don Rodrigue, and the
two scenes which follow, show the importance of symbolical
language and gestures and the expressionism of certain attitudes. The room in which the interview takes place is a
monastic cell with a black curtain at the bottom of it, which
was previously used as a torture chamber—and the instruments
of torture are still on the walls. The presence of Prouhèze,
who remains behind the curtain, dominates the scene. She
repulses Rodrigue and chooses to stay with Camille. Rodrigue
is completely humiliated by Camille, who tells him what he
might have done—he ought to have stormed the place or he
ought not to have come. That is one way of defining Rodrigue
and showing us that he is neither a saint nor a ruthless condottieri:

Pour un saint ou pour un homme de l'espèce que vous
décriviez,
Tout est simple. L'esprit parle, le désir parle, c'est bien. En
avant! il n'y a plus qu'à lui obéir aussitôt.

(p. 948)

He has come and he will go away by himself, all alone; he
knew when he came what Prouhèze's reply would be; he called
her twice, not three times, for he knew that, faithful to the

[93]

symbolism of numbers, the third time Prouhèze would have come. He has come to receive from Prouhèze's hands the wound which will bleed until he has conquered the world and come to the gates of death. Here more than ever he appears as the hero born to perform impossible tasks, longing for things which he cannot have. But he has in himself the force which will enable him to rise to heaven. Camille, on the contrary, is damned, and he needs to be redeemed; only Prouhèze can do that; and Rodrigue understands the necessity and leaves Mogador knowing that Prouhèze will soon fall to Camille's desire.

Scenes Ten and Eleven, which follow, are the most moving and pathetic of the play. In the preceding scene Rodrigue's and Camille's shadows had co-mingled in the light of the sun, symbol of real, natural life; but once Prouhèze and Rodrigue have decided not to see each other and to accept separation on earth, before they go in their respective directions, their shadows merge into one under the light of the moon in a moment which gives them eternity. The moon is the symbol of the disembodied world, of the spiritual contrasted with the material world of the sun. Prouhèze and Rodrigue, for one moment, belong spiritually to each other, and that spiritual union which is permissible will give them Eternity.

> Maintenant je porte accusation contre cet homme et cette femme par qui j'ai existé une seconde seule pour ne plus finir et par qui j'ai été imprimée sur la page de l'éternité!
> Car ce qui a existé une fois fait partie pour toujours des archives indestructibles.
>
> (p. 952)

Part Two

In Scene One, the announcer describes the various parts of the world in which the action of *Le Soulier de Satin* takes place. He moves from Prague to the open sea, and Mogador, where Prouhèze sleeps under her tent, but we feel that such cinematographic effects are difficult to realize on the stage, and the scene is unconvincing. Scene Two shows a Don Rodrigue who has grown in stature and has become a great conqueror, a leader who can handle men; he can, whatever they feel—whether it is love or hatred—attach them to himself, and make them obey him. Scenes Three and Four, which contain Dona Prouhèze's conversation with her guardian angel and later her dialogue with Camille, sum up Claudel's theology and form the apex of the play. They contain the final answers to the problem which Claudel has sought to solve in *Partage de Midi*, *L'Otage* and *L'Annonce faite à Marie*. They deal with the problem of love between man and woman and their relationship with their Maker. We have noted before how soon we passed from drama to tragedy and how we ceased to live in an atmosphere of suspense and tension leading to the *dénouement*, to be immersed in the pathos of two souls innocent, worthy of human happiness, and yet destined to illustrate by their suffering the ways of God to man. We have indeed pathos, but pathos of a certain kind, surely not the pathos of Greek tragedy, in which the audience could give its full sympathy to the innocent hero crushed by fate or by the whims of the gods. Here in this Christian world we know, for we are explicitly told so, that whatever happens on earth, whatever suffering takes place, is for the Supreme Good in Eternity; we know that Prouhèze will be a saint who will bring eternal bliss to Rodrigue and to Camille. And if one believes in a Heaven and in God's eternal bliss, how could one fail to envy the fate of those who at the cost of a few transient twinges reach that lasting holy state? One might, of course, feel completely repelled by the idea of a God-Fisherman who hauls His creatures to Him with a hook in their hearts; and as for those who do not believe in God, the whole thing can only appear as incomprehensible and barren of tragic emotions.

Leaving out Scenes Seven and Eight, which are of no importance, we come to Scene Nine, the only scene of the whole play where the two lovers, Prouhèze and Rodrigue, are at last, and for the first and only time, face to face. They know their tragic fate, and they can feel the weight of the Divine hand on their heads; they know that they cannot belong to each other, neither in the flesh nor even in spirit, for God does not permit it. It is only by returning to Him a soul which will have preserved nothing of its former life that Prouhèze will be from then on Rodrigue's star. That is the conclusion of Claudel's theological thought; so they part at the foot of the Cross, and Prouhèze returns to Mogador and death, while Rodrigue sets off on the last lap of his journey, towards his fall from the heights, his Calvary before death and some kind of peace, and yet with his greatest longing remaining for ever unfulfilled.

The Epilogue

Scene One. The announcer, still in his circus-master style, describes the fate which has overtaken Rodrigue. He has been deprived of his former power, banned as a traitor, and has become the object of public scorn. There are few examples of greater falls. After having conquered the world for Spain, after having won his place in God's heart by his faith in the spirit and his sacrifice, there he lies, physically depleted by the loss of a leg, ground by his spiritual suffering, yet master of his pain, greater than his torturers, his figure rising to heights which only the great heroes and symbols of mankind have ever reached.

Scene Two, the last scene of the play, shows the final fate of Rodrigue, mocked by the mob, deprived of all earthly consolations, yet strong in his faith, and confident that his daughter will carry on the task of liberating God's Church on earth; and so he consents to spend his last moments on earth in the shade of that same church, performing the most menial tasks, as if to show that the greatest ideal can survive even in the lowest of human conditions, and that the highest glories of the earth can be reduced to nought.

So ends *Le Soulier de Satin*. Are we moved by the suffering and final plight of Rodrigue? In a vague way, yes. At least we feel that we should be moved, as we are moved by the similar plight of the heroes of Greek tragedies. But the similarity between Rodrigue or Prouhèze and the hero of a Greek tragedy is only a superficial one. The hero of a Greek tragedy is a myth, that is to say, a human being, a legend or a tradition embodying one of the affective knots of the human consciousness, something which is deeply felt and lived through by all men at all times, beyond the reach of complete logical expression. Prouhèze or Rodrigue are not myths but symbols

[96]

and allegorical figures of concepts and emotions which are part of a pattern whose guiding threads are obviously in the hands of the creative mind who has brought them to life. There are points when they touch the plane of real human life, but on the whole they are not human in the way in which, for instance, Œdipus is human in exteriorizing the suffering caused by forces which no human mind or hand could avert. Œdipus' plight can be in some ways the plight of every human being. The suffering of unsatisfied love endured by Prouhèze and Rodrigue, their sacrifice and destitution cause feelings which are shared by all and could be experienced by all men, but in this case, even in the most tense moments, we can never forget the fact that the human beings who live those feelings are strange blends of legend, history, and idea-emotions symbolized into persons who in the end have no organic life, and no affective wholeness, as myths have.

Claudel says that *Le Soulier de Satin* is a *résumé* of his whole poetic and dramatic work. This is indeed true, and to my mind that truth embodies both the outstanding aspects and the weaknesses of the work. Here we find the main themes of Claudel's poetry and drama reappearing and being given a final form which bears the imprint of Claudel's personality. We have the theme of the superman thirsting for power, as outlined in *Tête d'or*, and we have spread across it, and lifted to the heights where Claudel wants to see it, the great theme of *Partage de Midi* summed up in the epigraph to *Le Soulier de Satin*, the Portuguese proverb: *Deus escreve direito por linhas tortas*, and the words of St. Augustine: *Etiam peccata*. We find once again the whole of Claudel's imagery and symbolism, but we find something more—an attempt to produce a vast synthesis which, although it is situated at a certain moment in time, is an apotheosis of the Catholic religion and its achievements on earth and a glorification of the main tenets of its dogma. That attempt could be partly accounted for by the maturation of Claudel's personality, and by his desire to communicate to others in a concrete form the answers which he has at last found in reply to questions which have certainly tormented his soul for a long time. He has by now reached certitudes, he is beyond the struggle between human love and the Divine Law which forms the texture of *Partage de Midi*, now he knows the ways of the Saint. There is grandeur in such visions, in such a splendid faith in oneself and the ways of the Maker, but there is also an inherent artistic weakness. Instead of allowing the action to take its course according to the various characters of the *dramatis personæ*, instead of allowing the poetry to rise from the events and from the genuine feelings of the characters, since the end is known in advance, both to us and to the mind which unfolds the drama, there is an inevitable tendency to force the characters into channels which have been prepared for them and which they must follow. This results in a lowering of dramatic tension and a weakening of the poetic expression which is no longer a spontaneous emanation of organically living characters, but bears definite marks of the passionate eloquence and convictions of the author.

Le Soulier de Satin is indeed in more than one way a summing up of Claudel's dramatic career. It is an exhilarating piece of writing, a vast Calderonian comedy, the scene of which embraces the world, and an attempt to sum up a whole aspect of the life of human society. The result is very impressive, but the didactic purpose is too apparent. *Le Soulier de Satin* is an attempt to produce a synthesis in a genre which cannot accept such a synthesis. One cannot make drama by trying to bring together various abstractions and by attempting to synthesize historical movements, actions, and creeds into dramatic characters. Dramatic characters must live, and those of *Le Soulier de Satin* do not live; they are part of a vast design, but they remain abstractions; they roam the world, but remain unconvincing. They are too much like puppets tied to strings hanging from clouds which every now and then are torn apart, allowing us to see the gigantic hand which moves them about, and we recognize this hand as that of Claudel or of God. Indeed, in this case there is no difference; Claudel speaks for both.

One of Claudel's errors is to believe that because he involves the universe, because his heroes encompass the world and juggle with it as if it were a globe in a study, he has widened the scope of the drama. In fact, he only widens the field of his eloquence, but he does not increase the tension which makes drama. Rodrigue is that enormous man who says:

> Ce n'est pas pour devenir à mon tour silence et immobilité que j'ai rompu un continent en deux et que j'ai passé deux mers. C'est parce que je suis catholique, c'est pour que toutes les parties de l'humanité soient réunies.

And after America he conquers Asia, and he would have taken over England had the King of Spain accepted his offer. The whole of Europe is brought together by Don Juan of Austria, the son of Dona Musique and of the Viceroy of Naples, and the dream of Prouhèze to hold Africa for the faith is continued by the expedition of Juan of Austria and his daughter, Marie de Sept-épées, whom we see at the end of the play, sailing towards Lepanto. The symbolism is obvious, the whole world is united into a Catholic synthesis.

After the battle of the White Mountain we find gathered in Prague all the great saints of Christianity—St. Boniface from the Saxon lands, and St. Denys from Greece; the Black Monk Luther has to be held at bay. Practically every great historical event has been forced into this drama in an attempt to produce a vast panorama of Catholic achievement. Even Napoleon's name has to come in, although he lived two centuries after the time when the action is supposed to take place; it may, of course, have been another Napoleon; still, he is called great, and history has known only one great Napoleon. Everything is there: the Armada sailing to England, and the rest of the fleet sailing to Lepanto; there is Queen Elizabeth and there is Mary Stuart. The desire to bring everything in is too pronounced, the symbolism too evident. Rodrigue is a symbolic hero who represents the Catholic desire to embrace the whole world, and he tries to conquer it materially and spiritually. He does not lack grandeur, and we cannot but be carried away by his splendid vision of one world:

> C'est pour qu'il n'y ait pas de trou que j'ai essayé d'élargir la terre. Le mal se fait toujours dans un trou.
> On fait le mal dans un trou, on ne le fait pas dans une cathédrale.
> (p. 822, vol. II)

How can we fail to be moved by an ideal of world unity? In days when that unity seems to be the only alternative to annihilation, we can only subscribe to it, and yet we cannot recognize it as part and parcel of the play. Rodrigue is the superman, the hero, so great as to be the symbol of all heroes, including the saint. The King of Spain, who sits in Madrid and directs that conquest of the world by the Catholic faith, knows it when he says:

> LE ROI: Tant pis! Lui-même l'a voulu, je ne vois aucun moyen de l'épargner.
> Je veux lui fourrer d'un seul coup dans le coeur tant de combustible qu'il en ait pour toute la vie!
> Au-dessus de ce monde là-bas qui est en proie à l'autre, d'un monde à l'état de bouillonnement et de chaos, au milieu de cet énorme tas de matière toute croulante et incertaine,
> Il me faut une àme absolument incapable d'être étouffée, il me faut un tel feu qu'il consume en un instant toutes les tentations comme de la paille,
> Nettoyé pour toujours de la cupidité et de la luxure.
> Je me plais à ce coeur qui brûle et à cet esprit dévorant, à ce grief éternel qui ne laisse à l'esprit point de repos.
> Oui, s'il n'y avait pas eu cet amour, il m'aurait fallu y suppléer moi-même par quelque grande injustice.
> (p. 655, vol. II)

As a first test Rodrigue has to conquer and to mould the newly-born continent of America; yet we know all too well that such an historical personage never existed. It is not a matter of taking liberties with history; we know and we agree that a play is not history, and that what counts is the poetic reality of the personages, but there are limits even to the imaginative acceptance of certain concrete facts. We can invent or arrange incidents of Cæsar's life, but we cannot go as far as inventing a world-conqueror who never existed, without placing ourselves on the plane of fantasy, and here the historical claims are so precise and yet so violently opposed to what everybody knows that they depersonalize the character of Rodrigue and make of it an abstraction completely devoid of reality. In spite of what some of Claudel's fervent apologists say, there is no *total drama*; such an expression has no meaning.

Drama implies conflict of certain forces at a given time, and if it expands in time and place and contains, as it does here, various aspects of social life, it becomes an epic, which may be dramatic, but is not a drama. The Kingdom of Denmark looks like a pin-head when compared with the vast dominions over which Rodrigue rules; yet Hamlet lives while Rodrigue does not, because the latter has no depth, no individuality, and is merely a symbol. Neither can we call *Le Soulier de Satin* a poem, for besides the vast stretches which have nothing to do with poetry, owing to the very nature of the work which was intended to be a drama, there is no unifying force which holds the poem together. The analogy of the *Divina Commedia* is not valid. There the poet, through his supreme imagination, welds together the contingent and the transcendent in an attempt to lift himself to the level of the Ideal, which links him with the Eternal, and he is the poem. In *Le Soulier de Satin* Rodrigue and Prouhèze have high ideals, which lead them both to sainthood, but they are only part of vast plans for the glorification of a great creed, and both are only means to that end. Prouhèze is the means of bringing Rodrigue to the gates of Heaven, Rodrigue is worthy of her and endures everything in order to reach sainthood, to which he is predestined. They may come near enough to sin and evil, but we know that they will not yield, that God will prevail, and that certitude saps the dramatic spring of the action. In fact, the character of the saint is not made for drama, but for mystery-plays. We know that in certain ways saints are made of a substance different from that of common mortals, but we know also— and this is what counts—from the dramatic point of view— that their suffering is part of a process which refines them for Eternity. We tremble in awe, and pray that one day perhaps the Divine Grace may lift us out of ourselves, but we realize that such characters have nothing to do with drama. It is not the determinism of the motives which destroys the drama, it is the triumphant certitude of the end.

Phèdre also is overwhelmed by a ruthless determinism, but in her we witness the harrowing struggle of a human being against forces which are bound to crush her, we are not aware that what takes place is for her good, and we can only suffer and sympathize with her fate, which is that of a being who pays for crimes for which she is not responsible. With Claudel there is no absolute struggle between good and evil. Evil is only part of the good, a means to the good; it is analogous to the Stoic grandeur of the Corneillian heroes who do not know evil, and experience conflicts of duties only in a theatre which involves a morality without religion. In Claudel the immanence and omnipresence of God reduce evil to the Spinozan concept of a part of the great whole:

> Qu'importe le désordre et la douleur d'aujourd'hui puis-qu'elle est le commencement d'autre chose, puisque
> Demain existe, puisque la vie continue, cette démolition avec nous des immenses réserves de la création,
> Puisque la main de Dieu n'a pas cessé son mouvement qui écrit avec nous sur l'éternité en lignes courtes ou longues,
> Jusqu'aux virgules, jusqu'au point le plus imperceptible,
> Ce livre qui n'aura son sens que quand il sera fini.

This brings me to a problem which however abstruse must, I feel, be faced. It is the problem of Claudel's theology and its intrusion into his drama. Right from the very beginning, the prayers of the Jesuit Father state in unmistakable terms the theme of the play:

> Mais, Seigneur, il n'est pas si facile de Vous échapper, et s'il ne va pas à Vous par ce qu'il a de clair, qu'il y aille par ce qu'il a d'obscur; et par ce qu'il a de direct, qu'il y aille par ce qu'il a d'indirect; et par ce qu'il a de simple,
> Qu'il y aille par ce qu'il a en lui de nombreux, et de laborieux et d'entremêlé,
> Et s'il désire le mal, que ce soit un tel mal qu'il ne soit compatible qu'avec le bien,
> Et s'il désire le désordre, un tel désordre qu'il implique l'ébranlement et la fissure de ces murailles autour de lui qui lui barraient le salut,
> Je dis à lui et à cette multitude avec lui qu'il implique ob-scurément.
>
> (p. 860)

We are told all along that the woman is going to be once more, as in *Partage de Midi*, the instrument of salvation, God's bait, which will hook and drag the human heart to Him. Now this image of the woman as a 'jack' or as a 'hook' which God

uses as a bait, implies a cruelty which does not befit God. I
do not take it literally, but I cannot accept it even figuratively.
I cannot conceive the idea of God's deliberately using the
suffering of His creatures in order to lift them or others to Him.
I am aware that any kind of revelation implies suffering, I am
aware that any attempt to probe the sources of Being entails
pain, great pain, and even more, sometimes moral suffering
greater than the human heart can endure without a break-up
of the human frame, I am aware that in order to make contact
with God, in order to have a possible revelation of the great
truth, man must remain ever vulnerable, prepared to suffer
armed with the single conviction that the light which he shall
see is worth any suffering, but I cannot conceive of a God
deliberately imposing suffering on any one of His creatures,
even if this be for the greater good. I shall go further: I
believe in metaphysical determinism, I believe that anything
that happens has to happen, and can only happen that way, I
believe that we are part of an immense pattern, and that it is
not within our power either to change that pattern or to alter
the course we have been set upon, I believe that Life flows
inexorably and inevitably from a beginning, and that the end
for the Supreme Eye is already there and cannot be changed
by human will. In short, I do not believe in absolute free will,
in metaphysical free will, and life, which is both good and evil,
is within God's Will. Perhaps evil is only part of existence,
perhaps it is that very act of passing from non-being to being
which entails a certain evil, for it brings about a break in the
purity and absolute harmony of non-being. But although
I conceive evil as being perhaps within God's original will in
the passage from Eternity to Time, and from Time to Eternity,
I cannot conceive of God closely following every one of His
creatures and submitting them individually to evil in order to
produce a greater good. That, to me, is a form of human
cruelty which I cannot ascribe to God. Evil is part of life,
part of the great pattern, and as such must be accepted, but
it does not imply the actual will of the Transcendence. In my
view Transcendence which is accessible to prayer intervenes
only to do good, and never for evil, which is immanent and
not transcendent.

Faust's life, for instance, is not righteous in any of its parts, and yet in the end righteousness is accepted for the whole. The faults of Faust in Time are blessings in disguise, and in the end grace redeems for eternity what was imperfect and insufficient in Time. As Spinoza says, ' A thing is seen within the form of Eternity, when all its parts or stages are conceived in their time relations and thereby conceived together '. The blots in Faust's life were necessary blots, yet Mephistopheles, the tempter and main agent of the plot, is not part of God's plan, he appears as something beyond God's Will, a necessary evil of Creation perhaps, a force which is outside God's original pattern, and yet sprung from it, and therefore tolerated as a part of a system which tests man's sense of personal responsibility. I believe in Grace for lifting the being, I do not believe in Grace in reverse. God's intervention through actual Grace can only be an act of love, which cannot imply any torment of a human creature, even for the sake of another's good. Although the person who receives God's Grace—the saint, for instance—cannot of course avoid human suffering, which is part of the process of sainthood, for one must renounce all human possessions, in order to be completely free and to be received in God, I do not believe that when God's Grace comes to a creature whom He wishes to lift to Him, He chooses at the same time the persons who are going to suffer in order to make that operation possible. God is love, and suffering, though part of life, is beyond His actual will, but possibly within His original will, the will which created life. But life is a process which God Himself cannot now reverse until it has reached the end which He has Himself fixed. These views may be very personal, but they sometimes prevent me from identifying myself completely with Claudel's poetry.

There is no need to elaborate further the relationship between belief and artistic creation; it seems to me that I. A. Richards and above all T. S. Eliot, in his essay on Dante, have spoken words of wisdom which throw a clear light on the problem. We can indeed read and enjoy Dante or Milton without sharing their religious beliefs, but in the case of a writer who, like Claudel, makes of them the kernel of his artistic creations,

there is no ' suspension of belief ', and very often in Claudel's
works one finds oneself inevitably confronted with the choice
between accepting or refusing his theology as a prerequisite
to the enjoyment of some of his creations. For the enthusiastic
Claudelian, that theology is part of his greatness, but I humbly
confess that it proves for me an insuperable stumbling-block.
I cannot accept, for instance, the idea of a God-chosen people,
and the idea that faith is propagated by force; I cannot forget
that Christ chided Peter when he drew his sword in His
defence; I cannot forget that His innocence, His all-embracing
love were His defence, and I cannot accept such views as:
*ce qui est beau réunit, ce qui est beau vient de Dieu. Je ne puis
l'appeler autrement que Catholique.* It seems to me that by now
the old Hebraic conception of God as the scourge of His enemies
should be truly dead, and replaced by the conception of the
God of Love, the God whose supreme will embraces the world,
and who cannot possibly approve of the conversion of Islam
or other ' heretics ' by means of the sword. The ages of the
crusades are long past, and the Omnipotent can only be the
All-merciful.

This brief incursion into theology seems to me necessitated
by the very nature of the play, which is, above all, a vast
synthesis of Catholicism and its achievements; the very souls
of the various European nations are explained in terms of
Catholicism. The Third Journey begins with scenes of epic
grandeur and of obvious symbolism. Juan of Austria has
marched into Bohemia in order to stem the onslaught of the
enemies of Christendom; the scene which follows—the
vision of Spain, her traditions and her gigantic struggles as the
defender of the Faith—is reminiscent of the Victor Hugo of
Ruy Blas, but definitely to the advantage of Claudel, who shows
a superb sense of the colossal and cosmic, and at the same time
a very profound sense of the human. We not only have
broad historical frescoes, we also have a definite feeling of
life; there we can see the countless barbarian migrations
swaying to and fro across Europe, we can see all the physical
and spiritual foes marshalled against a chosen cause; and we
realize that not only is Claudel's theology as such difficult to
accept, but also that the application of some of its tenets to

dramatic art makes drama impossible. The main protagonists of the drama, in as far as Prouhèze's and Rodrigue's love is part of the drama, have no freedom of action, and that lack of freedom is not due to an inner compulsion but to definite manifestations of Divine power. One may say that Divine power can manifest itself only through the consciousness of its existence based in the soul, but in the case which concerns us we find ourselves faced with the application of one of the most serious aspects of the Christian dogma, which differentiates between intuitive revelation of the Divine and the definite manifestation of the Divine will to the human creature. From the beginning Prouhèze pledges herself, in her beautiful prayer to the Virgin, that she will not fail, and asks that should she forget her prayers, the Divine presence should intervene every time, whenever it is required; and her prayer is heard and accepted; when Rodrigue goes to meet her, he is seriously wounded in defence of St. Jacques' church, and when Prouhèze's will wavers, her guardian angel is always at hand to keep her to her normal level of Corneillian heroism or rather, predestined sainthood.

The scene where the moon speaks sets out once and for all the kind of relationship which we can expect between the two lovers. Their love, in order to transcend death, must remain an ideal love within the law. The double shadow is the pure being formed by the ideal union of Rodrigue and Prouhèze in Eternity, and their love can only exist there and nowhere else:

> Oui, je sais qu'il ne m'épousera que sur la croix et nos âmes l'une à l'autre dans la mort et dans la nuit hors de tout motif humain!
> Si je ne puis être son paradis, du moins je puis être sa croix! Pour que son âme avec son corps y soit écartelée je vaux bien ces deux morceaux de bois qui se traversent!
> Puisque je ne puis lui donner le ciel, du moins je puis l'arracher à la terre. Moi seule puis lui fournir une insuffisance à la mesure de son désir!
> Moi seule étais capable de le priver de lui-même.
> Il n'y a pas une région de son âme et pas une fibre de son corps dont je ne sente qu'elle est faite pour être fixée à moi, il n'y a rien dans son corps et dans cette âme qui a fait son corps

que je ne sois capable de tenir avec moi pour toujours dans le
sommeil de la douleur,
Comme Adam, quand il dormit, la première femme.

(p. 681)

Here we have one of the key passages of the play, and above
all we have what is surely great poetry, the kind of poetry whose
moving beauty and cosmic range reach to the very sources of
Being. I do not think that there is anywhere in *Le Soulier de
Satin* more beautiful poetry than this meditation of the moon,
and it is a meditation which derives a great deal of its pathos
from the fact that it is congruent to the play, and contributes
to the knowledge of the main characters. It lifts the lovers
to a plane above the human and it shows them as part of a
vast design in which they retain some of their moving humanity.
The action continues with Rodrigue in front of Mogador, and
when he wonders what to do, the hulk of the old boat ' Santiago ' surges to the surface of the sea and reminds him of the
great benevolent presence of St. James, who watches over his
destiny. Had his will failed, Prouhèze's will would not have
failed, for the guardian angel who had visited her when asleep
in her tent on the shore had succeeded in screwing her courage
up to the final pitch of self-sacrifice and sainthood. That scene
is the central scene, one of the most moving of the play, and a
high-water mark of poetry in the play. There the guardian
angel, with the image of the revolving globe casting its shadow
on the tent, explains to the full the implications of the words
of the Jesuit Father at the beginning of the play, and the
meaning of Claudelian theology. Here we learn that the
loved being exists not by himself, but only in the *loved one*, in
order to make him what he is destined to be, and not what the
others would like him to be, or what he himself would like to be.
This is a point of view which undoubtedly implies predestination and grace. By accepting the Law, the being reaches
Eternity, and in order to reach Eternity also the other being can
only wish for death. But before death, and in order to be
able to offer her soul to God, and therefore in order to be able
to live in Eternity with Rodrigue, Prouhèze must claim her
soul back from him and renounce all in order to have all
eternally.

H

At this point Christian theology meets the longing for the unattainable and for death of all the Romantic heroes. Here we have a superb unfolding of the mysterious ways of God in beautiful poetry, but it is more of a ritual than a dramatic scene; we watch the image of Prouhèze's fate, we learn through her dialogue with her guardian angel about God's unfathomed ways; but we are, I think, more awed by the breath-taking contrast between the finite and the infinite, by those glimpses of the Eternal and of the ways to reach it, than moved by the suffering of the human beings involved. We cannot pity them, we cannot suffer for them, for theirs is the state which every true believer should hope to reach, and the non-believer will, I am afraid, find the whole thing difficult to comprehend. The predestination is evident, the guardian angel already holds in his hands the stone which is to be the cause of the shipwreck of Rodrigue's boat, the revolving globe shows the lands and seas which Rodrigue is going to cross, the labours he is going to perform, and the scene ends with the immense image of the Immaculate Conception stretching across the sky. It is a beautiful scene, difficult to portray in extracts:

Je suis Agar dans le désert! Sans mains, sans yeux, il y a quelqu'un qui m'a rejoint amèrement dans le désert!

C'est le désir qui étreint le désespoir! C'est l'Afrique par-dessus la mer qui épouse les terres empoisonnées du Mexique!

Dona Prouhèze: Eh quoi! Ainsi c'était permis? Cet amour des créatures l'une pour l'autre, il est donc vrai que Dieu n'en est pas jaloux? l'homme entre les bras de la femme. . . .

L'Ange Gardien: Comment serait-Il jaloux de ce qu'Il a fait? et comment aurait-Il rien fait qui ne lui serve?

Dona Prouhèze: L'homme entre les bras de la femme oublie Dieu.

L'Ange Gardien: Est-ce l'oublier que d'être avec Lui? est-ce ailleurs qu'avec Lui d'être associé au mystère de Sa création,

Franchissant de nouveau pour un instant l'Eden par la porte de l'humiliation et de la mort?

Dona Prouhèze: L'amour hors du sacrement n'est-il pas le péché?

L'Ange Gardien: Même le péché! Le péché aussi sert.

Dona Prouhèze: Ainsi il était bon qu'il m'aime?
L'Ange Gardien: Il était bon que tu lui apprennes le désir.

(pp. 720, 721)

This symbolical scene is followed by the scene between Prouhèze and Camille which completes the exposition of Claudel's theology. Here we have confirmation of the idea that the good and the bad are instruments of the greater Power, and therefore we are entitled to think that the bad ones have perhaps as much right to be admired and accepted as the good ones. Camille is used to bring Prouhèze to the place where she must go, but it could have been the other way round; both are part of the same ' necessity ', and although we may for a brief moment, when Camille bullies Prouhèze, forget that necessity and sympathize with the sufferer, we are soon made aware of the fact that Camille performs, like every-body else in the play, his appointed task, and that Prouhèze will save him as well as Rodrigue; in fact, he begs her to do so, for although grace has not yet touched him, he knows what it is, recognizing it in Prouhèze, and he asks her to use it in his favour, just as Mara had asked Violaine to save her; and so in the end Camille appears as one of the means of raising Prouhèze to sainthood. It is he who tells her, ruthlessly, that although Rodrigue is the cross upon which she is nailed, she can be his star only if she banishes him from her mind, and thinks solely of God:

Don Camille: Prouhèze, quand vous priez, êtes-vous toute à Dieu? et quand vous Lui offrez ce coeur tout rempli de Rodrigue, quelle place Lui reste-t-il?

Dona Prouhèze, *sourdement*: Il suffit de ne point faire le mal. Dieu demande-t-Il que pour Lui nous renoncions à toutes nos affections?

Don Camille: Faible réponse! Il y a les affections que Dieu a permises et qui sont une part de Sa Volonté.
Mais Rodrigue dans votre coeur n'est aucunement effet de Sa Volonté mais de la vôtre. Cette passion en vous.

Dona Prouhèze: La passion est unie à la croix.

Don Camille: Quelle croix?

Dona Prouhèze: Rodrigue est pour toujours cette croix à laquelle je suis attachée.

[109]

Don Camille: Pourquoi donc ne lui laissez-vous pas achever son oeuvre?

Dona Prouhèze: Ne revient-il pas du bout du monde pour l'achever?

Don Camille: Mais vous n'acceptez la mort de sa main que pour rendre par là votre âme de lui plus proche.

Dona Prouhèze: Tout ce qui en moi est capable de souffrir la croix, ne le lui ai-je pas abandonné?

Don Camille: Mais la croix ne sera satisfaite que quand elle aura tout ce qui en vous n'est pas la volonté de Dieu détruit.

(pp. 743, 744, vol. II)

This is the supreme renunciation, the gesture of the saint. It is difficult to reconcile all those conflicting things as part of God's Will. One wonders if God needs such examples to enlighten the others. Just as Mara asks Violaine, Camille asks Prouhèze to be a saint and to save him, and in both cases charity triumphs, as in the Redemption. But although we feel that the gesture is great, the drama disappears, and the only thing that remains is the symbolical value of the scene.

The scene which follows and which, for the first and only time, brings Rodrigue and Prouhèze together, reaches sublime heights. There is, of course, a great deal of rhetoric and theological argumentation, and there is the weak aspect of the characters, the tendency to make of these two lovers the quintessence of all lovers, from Tristram and Iseult to Antony and Cleopatra. The difference between these legendary heroes and those of *Le Soulier de Satin* is that the former had, all of them, a very definite reality, a tangible form on earth, and they were made of flesh and blood, while the latter appear too much the expression of a dogma and the means of a theological demonstration. We know that Prouhèze could never give herself to Rodrigue, and she knows it, she who has heard and approved her husband saying:

Ce que Dieu a joint l'homme ne peut le séparer,
Cela qu'elle m'a donné, je ne pourrais le lui rendre quand je le
    voudrais.

All the characters of *Le Soulier de Satin* know that they are in God's hands, and in spite of the fact that they know they are destined to each other in Eternity, as were all the other extraordinary pairs of lovers, Prouhèze and Rodrigue also know that they must accept their fate, which consists in not belonging to each other, and in making of that predestined love the means to reach sainthood. Prouhèze knows that if ever she transgressed the Law as did Francesca da Rimini with Paolo, she could only give Rodrigue the desire of the damned, and not the pure love of Beatrice, which she knows is meant to be hers. We are driven back again to that Claudelian belief which implies the use of the woman and the awareness of sin as a means of salvation:

> Pour les uns l'intelligence suffit. C'est l'esprit qui parle purement à l'esprit.
> Mais pour les autres il faut, que la chair aussi peu à peu soit évangelisée et convertie. Et quelle chair pour parler à l'homme plus puissante que celle de la femme?

We are back to the old insoluble problem—how can this desire be evil, if it is part of a pre-ordained order of things beyond man? And together with this, we have a second problem which presents a similar intractability—the problem of the relationships between body and soul. We are faced here with the conception that, while the soul is the unique thing which may, through some mysterious correspondence, be linked with another soul, flesh is the common element without any character of uniqueness, and which must be transcended in order to reach the higher order. This is a difficult point, for it implies a separation between body and soul, a separation which has in fact been rejected by many Christian thinkers, and is contradicted by the dogma of Resurrection and the Assumption of the Blessed Virgin. Surely the body is as much God's work as the soul, and an individuation of the soul in Eternity presupposes the existence of a certain substance which may well have existed or may exist again in Time. From the point of view of drama, that dissociation between body and soul and the knowledge that what we see on earth is only the shadow of actions which take place beyond, together with the fact that from the very beginning we know that under Divine guidance the characters can only reach their appointed ends, weaken the dramatic tension and tend to reduce the characters to abstractions. Prouhèze knows that she is God's instrument, and that she alone can open for Rodrigue the gates of Heaven, so she never sees Rodrigue, except when, after her life of suffering on earth, she is about to die, and she leaves him with her daughter, who, strangely enough, in an immaculate way, is also his, and when she already sees herself in the sky as the star which will guide his way.

Le Soulier de Satin is not truly a drama, except perhaps in the way in which Calderon's baroque comedies are called drama. It is a hybrid of the miracle- and mystery-play, but also an enormous creation worthy of Claudel, who is a huge man, a man of genius, who can sing with an harmonious orphic voice or shatter us with a Cyclopean roar. It is a work which contains wonderful things, flights into realms of great poetry and patches which look like sack on silk. Take the so-called comic of Claudel, for instance, which is probably meant to convey that kind of universality, of fulness of life which we find in Shakespeare's plays; the trouble is that those grotesque interludes which Claudel has introduced seem to have been brought in merely because they are part of the recipe, but they do not add a jot to the drama, which is better without them. The fool in *Lear*, the grave-diggers in *Hamlet* are not interludes in the action; on the contrary, they heighten the dramatic tension by prolonging it and by giving it, so to speak, time to rebound to greater heights. One has to gather breath in order to continue those vertiginous ascents. In Claudel those comic scenes are not out of tone, but they are irrelevant, they are interesting writing, but they are not part of the drama. There are many other things which do not fit, and which seem to be there for Claudel's merriment—the dance of the black girl, naked in the moonlight, is a flight into fantasy which is out of the real experience of the drama; then there is the enormous machinery required to bring the world on to the stage; there is the weakness inherent in the part of the narrator, who, being the link between the audience and the stage, introduces grotesque elements when they are least expected, and also a magic-carpet atmosphere (as when he brings together Prouhèze and Rodrigue's mother) which would be acceptable in a fairy tale or in a puppet-show, but not in drama.

We have in *Le Soulier de Satin* an expressionism which is not alien to Claudel, but which is probably more marked in this play than in others. Certain poses of the human figures are forced, like the El Greco pose of the man who holds the gilded statue of the Virgin at the entrance to Don Pélage's house, and we have the striking contrast of colours, black and white, and the dark green or red, which symbolize all the violence of Spain. But, above all, the *dramatis personæ* are too symbolical, they are not characters but the representations of abstractions, perhaps types; their speech is very symbolical and often ends in sheer eloquence, and their actions are even more symbolical, and meant to bring to mind memories of some of the greatest events in Christian religion. It is only in that light that we can understand them, and it is only in that context that they acquire a moving greatness. Three times Prouhèze struggled against the bushes before she fell at the feet of her guardian angel. Then we have the symbolism of her struggle with the angel, and of course side by side with it the symbolism of the life of Rodrigue, who, like Christ, conquered the world and was brought to death amidst derision and suffering.

But those restrictive remarks are not meant to detract from the fact that *Le Soulier de Satin* is a work which shows the full maturity of Claudel's poetic genius. His visionary power, his cosmic range, are unparalleled in our time. Claudel is the master of vast visions, he is the man whose imagination can embrace continents and enclose them into images of extraordinary concreteness and explosive force. Let us take his description of Africa:

> La terre ne serait point ce qu'elle est si elle n'avait ce carreau de feu sur le ventre, ce cancer rongeur, ce rayon qui lui dévore le foie, ce trépied attisé par le souffle des océans, cet antre fumant, ce fourneau où vient se dégraisser l'ordure de toutes les respirations animales,
>
> (p. 579, vol. II)

or the image of America stretched like a bow between the poles, or the bird's-eye view of the glories of Spain and the Faith, or the sensuousness of the images and the depth of feeling which emerge from the moving meditations of the moon, and we shall easily realize that Claudel's poetic genius has certain features which are unique in our time.

VII

L'OTAGE, LE PAIN DUR, LE PÈRE HUMILIÉ

WE come now to a trilogy of plays which have a semi-historical, or should we say a pseudo-historical foundation, and whose action should have something of the force which carried forward Greek tragedies; Claudel was, at the time when he wrote them, translating Aeschylus' *Orestia.* At first sight these three tragedies may seem to be a new departure in Claudel's dramatic work; indeed, the action is situated in history and deals with personages who are well known and who are in fact very close to our time. Yet as soon as one enters the core of the plays one realizes that the theme is once again the old, Claudelian theme of God's ways with His creatures, which spans his whole dramatic output from beginning to end; and here, as in most of Claudel's plays, the theme dominates the material which he uses, whether human or historical, and sometimes with not altogether happy results. The *ananke* of the Greeks is here replaced by the determinism of history and of human passions. Claudel and his enthusiastic admirers would certainly deny that any suggestion of metaphysical determinism could be attached to his plays, yet the unavoidable developments and the conclusions which take place once certain forces are set in motion, evidence a belief in historical determinism which, in the transcendental atmosphere of Claudel's plays, implies metaphysical determinism. The end of an historical movement is contained in its beginning, and follows as ineluctably as death follows birth. The explanation that an historical movement comes to an end because of a failure to remain faithful to the forces which brought it into being can only mean that the seed of failure was part of the whole, for if that element of failure could not be traced to forces which by various processes go back to the beginning, how else could that element have been

[115]

introduced into the movement, except by the act of an extraneous will stronger than man's will?

L'Otage

Act I, Scene I, introduces two of the main characters of the play—Sygne and Coûfontaine—and localizes the action. Napoléon's armies are bogged in the depths of Russia; the legitimist cause still has many active supporters—George de Coûfontaine is one of them. Forsaken by his wife before she died, having lost all his family and the land of his ancestors, his loyalty to his dethroned King is his only faith. Sygne, his cousin, like him a Coûfontaine, shares his ideals, his desire to restore the King to his throne and with him the old order, which for them made the greatness of France, yet with something more, for Sygne believes in God. Instead of leading the adventurous life of her cousin, she has set herself the task of wresting back bit by bit from the Revolutionaries the land and properties which they had seized. She devotes her energy to immediate tasks and to the propagation of good around her. At the end of the scene, the two cousins make a solemn pledge to remain faithful to each other, and never to belong to anyone else. The only disagreement between the two is about God, in Whom Sygne firmly believes.

Scene II. The Pope and Coûfontaine. Coûfontaine wishes the Pope to take sides and to follow the King of France in his exile to England. The Pope refuses, and although he has been rescued from Napoléon's soldiers by Coûfontaine, he maintains that his place is in Rome among his people, even if he were compelled to live in the Catacombs. Coûfontaine passionately believes in his lost feudal world, in the idea of the King giving life to the world of God, which for him is an abstraction. For him society is based on a tradition and an order which gives to everyone his proper place in a pattern which stretches from the King to the meanest of his subjects. Now the *Law* has become the new idol, and force has, according to him, replaced sacrifice. This scene, which does not lack dramatic value, shows Coûfontaine's inability to realize the changes which have taken place, the force of the historical necessity which has brought them about, and the pressing need to try to effect a reconciliation between the old and the new, so that a society which contains both may continue to live.

Act II, Scene I, presents the first clash between the two opposites—Sygne and Turelure. Turelure the revolutionary, who has achieved power and success, realizes that the violence of the beginning, which was perhaps necessary, should now give way to compromise and to a marriage of what remains of the old traditions with the new. In spite of his pride and his violence, he has not been able to forget that he belongs to the slave race, and that it is only through marriage that he can have access to the master race; therefore he proposes marriage to Sygne. He comes to her with certain trump cards in his hands—he knows that Coûfontaine and the Pope are within his reach, and he knows that Sygne's sense of duty will, in the end, transcend her abhorrence and personal hatred of him. Sygne emerges from that scene with the character of a young woman of perfect self-control and undauntable courage.

Scene II. Sygne and Badilon. It is in this scene that Sygne's greatness appears, while the priest's arrogant dogmatism in compelling her to this most unhuman sacrifice appears to us as repellent and unacceptable on the Christian plane. This is the central scene of the play. The whole dramatic tension, which has been till now carefully built up, the problem of verisimilitude and sympathy between audience and characters, hinges on this scene, and one feels compelled to say that, whether on the theological or on the dramatic plane, the scene is unacceptable and leaves one with a feeling of indefinable horror. One cannot help thinking of the pagan sacrifice of Iphegenia by her father, intent on pleasing ruthless gods. The arrogance of the priest, who without much hesitation borrows the voice of the Supreme Truth and the force of compulsion, is in no way founded on arguments which make either acceptable. Only Divine Grace could explain the transition from his acknowledged ignorance to the subtle, and in the end convincing, dialectics which he uses, and it is not possible to think that the infliction of such harrowing suicide on a pure being like Synge could be God's expressed will. The sacrifices that God demands from human beings are meant to lift our mortal natures up to a higher plane, and not to

defile them by unnatural compulsions which are a denial of
spiritual values. The Pope's life, contrary to what the priest
says, is not at stake; Turelure merely wants him back as his
former prisoner, but even if the Pope had to be put to death, as
God's Son was, his end would have brought more glory to God
and to the Faith than his salvation through unredeemable
sacrifices. As for Sygne's cousin George, he is a soldier prepared to die at any moment, and he would never have con-
sented to be saved by his cousin's dishonour. The whole scene
has too strong a flavour of ruthless paganism and cannot be
made to fit into the Christian climate in which it is situated.

Act III. The first scene, with Sygne and George, is very
moving; it is dramatic, poignant, and full of pathos, on account
of the undeserved reproaches which Sygne has to withstand.
The two characters seem to have been the toys of a most cruel
fate. George's sad complaint about his solitude, his suffering
following Sygne's betrayal, the reproaches which he addresses
to her, although harsh, are human, and spring from the depth
of his sorrow. Sygne has to accept them undeservedly with a
heart heavier than any of her cousin's words could make it.
Her plight and suffering call upon our pity and we feel that
death will be liberation for her. At this point we reach tragedy.

L'Otage is indeed a mixture of drama and tragedy. The first
half, comprising the dialogues between the Pope and Coûfontaine, those between Turelure and Sygne and between Sygne
and Badilon, is drama; after that the dramatic tension and
suspense are suddenly interrupted and replaced by the pathos
born from the sacrifice imposed on Sygne; we move then from
drama to tragedy. The means used are the means of Greek
tragedy—a blind, ruthless force which crushes an innocent
victim. Unfortunately for the play, this kind of compulsion
cannot be fitted into the atmosphere of Christian dogma, it
destroys the balance of forces, and the foundation of faith upon
which the play is grounded becomes the monstrous fatalism
which makes Badilon say:

> Tout est épuisé jusqu'au fond, tout est exprimé jusqu'à la
> dernière goutte.

and that by God's command—

. . . qui parlait par ma bouche, et qui entendait par vos oreilles.

Those are words which do not enable us to preserve our support and sympathy for Badilon.

In Claudel's conception of the cosmos the temporal and the eternal seem sometimes to be separated, and we seem to have prayer and Divine Grace in order to lift up human creatures unto God, but in fact there is no separation, and everything that happens to man—good or evil—is part of God's unchangeable plan. Turelure, the wretched Turelure, is also one of God's creatures, as Badilon the priest clearly says: *A lui aussi Dieu pense de toute éternité et il est Son très cher enfant.* Of course this is a very Christian conception, for, good or bad, we are indeed all God's children, though there may be degrees of ' dearness '. But a more serious problem is raised by the conception of human freedom embodied in Badilon's plea to Sygne's question: *Qu'attendez-vous de moi ?* and the reply is: *Cette chose pour laquelle il apparaît que vous avez été créée et mise au monde.* This is surely determinism, and of a kind which makes God responsible for human suffering. The scene has, to my mind, a masochistic flavour, and is repellent. The part played by the priest in expressing the hidden design of God, who in His supreme will has planned to extract the last ounce of moral suffering from one of His creatures, is odious. It is difficult to escape the dilemma of either profaning the great sacrament of marriage, which requires the wholeness of being in body and soul, or of denying the existence of the very soul itself through the fact that Sygne is requested, seems to have been born, to love devotedly and absolutely, according to God's Law in the holy sacrament of marriage, the very butcher of her father and mother. ' Love thine enemy '—yes; but that Divine Wisdom should be embodied into such sub-human, or perhaps super-human action, is difficult to accept. That saints and martyrs may have endured with an ethereal joy all kinds of sufferings for their faith is understandable, but the conception of the saint as the being whose soul must be, by God's specific design, crushed to dust, so that he may rise and henceforth live in God, is more than difficult to accept as a positive Christian belief.

[119]

Here we are beyond the theme of *Le Soulier de Satin*, where we found that the human creature can only love in God, or beyond the salvation of Mara by her victim—Violaine; for here there is no excuse for human jealousy, a motive which has sometimes caused the most violent actions, and sometimes called forth the most saintly responses; but here the complete oblation of a human soul is carried out in cold, very cold, blood. The dogmatism of the priest who takes upon himself to explain God's Will, the casuistry employed are repellent. Above all, the historical compulsion used in order to motivate Sygne's sacrifice is denied by history itself—that part of history which is too near us, and has been too well explored to leave us with the possibility of ' a suspension of belief ' necessary to the acceptance of the priest's casuistry, a casuistry which oscillates between hollow and high-flown rhetoric (*et les myriades humaines l'une sur l'autre, attendent votre résolution*) and a well-nigh unbearably insidious form of moral torture. One cannot help feeling that there is here something unfortunately daemonic, and which flavours of the Black Mass when Badilon says: *et moi votre prêtre, je me lève à mon tour et je me tiens au-dessus de cette victime immolée.*

Besides the unacceptability of the very principle of Sygne's sacrifice, Badilon's whole argument is also faulty, for it was not the first time that the Pope had been dragged out of Rome. Those very kings whom, in spite of the fact that they had destroyed his human happiness, G. de Coûfontaine seems to uphold in the name of ' the natural order ' had kept the Pope in Avignon for more than three score years. The fact that ' order ' without any other foundation than that of its existence is truly jungle law is of no importance to G. de Coûfontaine. In the end Sygne dies, killed by her cousin; her cousin dies, killed by Turelure, and we are left with the impression that there are deeds which weigh heavily on the responsibility of a God Who is terrible indeed: *Tout est fini, tout est fait comme il le fallait, l'épouse absoute est couchée dans ses vêtements nuptiaux. J'ai achevé mon oeuvre, j'ai achevé mon enfant pour le ciel. Et moi je reste seul,* says Badilon.

If we can get over the abhorrent theology and forget history, then we may feel that *L'Otage* has far more dramatic action than any other of Claudel's plays. Although it contains far less good poetry than the best plays, the dialogue is more dramatic and the building up of the atmosphere of the play, in the first scene of the first Act, for instance, constitutes a masterly exposition and contains good poetry. If one can accept its premises, the play is a combination of, at times, good drama and tragedy; but it seems to me that the events here described are still too recent, too well known to be twisted with advantage into the shapes which Claudel gives to them. This young woman, who is compelled to save Christendom, this Turelure who restores the King of France to his throne and arranges for the end of the play that ' *kolossal* ' yet repellent display of gold braids and human baseness, are characters whose existence is endangered by the unfounded historical claims which their creator makes for them. If we can uphold the symbolical value of certain historical events and characters as expressions and crystallizations of great historical movements, we cannot twist. or synthesize well-known historical events and characters into dramatic creations which could hope to have a life of their own.

Le Pain dur

Act I, Scene I, contains the exposition of the motives which actuate the two protagonists. Lumir, who is engaged to Turelure's son, wants Turelure to repay her the money which she has lent to his son; she needs it to give it back to Poland. Sichel wants Turelure to marry her. Turelure is therefore the lynch-pin of the whole situation. He is old and worn out, and a strong emotion could easily kill him. The scene which follows does not contribute anything to the development of characters, but Scene III is a very important one. Turelure tells Lumir that he will not give her back the money which she has lent to his son; Lumir is very distressed, and in the end she agrees to marry him on condition that he gives her back the money. The Act ends with a scene which shows that Sichel and Turelure are well matched in cunning. Turelure is ruthless in the satisfaction of his passion, Sichel is without any scruples and wants to attain her ends.

Act II begins with all the characters of the play gathered together in the first scene, which is of no importance. The scene which follows is the central scene of the play; there the action which will shape the course of the play is decided upon. Lumir, like Lady Macbeth, screws Louis's courage up to fighting point. Lumir is a fanatic possessed by a strong ideal and prepared to do anything for it. On the contrary, Louis is weak and vacillating, yet, lashed by Lumir's insults, lured by her beauty, he is in the end determined to act so as not to lose her. Scene III, which follows with Louis and Turelure, brings to mind memories of the *Agamemnon*, where Orestes avenges his father's murder upon his mother. Louis, the son of Sygne, avenges his mother. Turelure is a good gambler to the last; he does not lack courage, and he shows that he can remain to the end the adventurer who can face up to the most difficult situations. Louis fires a shot and Turelure dies of heart failure.

Act III begins with a scene without importance and with rather over-worked comic effects. The scene which follows, between Lumir and Louis, is a very moving one, and contains the best poetry of the play. It is a scene which does not lack tragic force. Lumir is the only true idealist of the play, the only one who realizes that *la vraie vie est absente*. She is the only one prepared to give up her life, her soul, everything she has, for an ideal. She could have loved Louis if he had been made of the same mettle, and had he been capable of rising to her level, but he can think only of earthly possessions, so she goes away alone to face her destiny. Louis, left by himself face to face with Sichel, could not fail to succumb to her determined will to marry him. She places herself at his mercy by destroying the documents which made her heir to part of Turelure's fortune, and Louis cannot but offer to marry her. She accepts, explaining that it will give her the means of shaking off the cares which weigh upon her race. One cannot but contrast Lumir's idealism with the bitterness and the feelings of anger which invade Sichel at the thought that she belongs to the oppressed race, and that the time has come to show the Gentiles that she is as good as any one of them. The play closes with Louis and Sichel's father, Ali, endeavouring to outdo each other through various bargains, and the final gestures of the end ripple away towards the symbol which widens the meaning of the play. Louis asks Ali to buy from him the image of Christ which, after having been battered to bits during the revolution, had been brought together again by Sygne. After some Judas-like bargaining, Ali accepts, and Louis the unbeliever strikes Christ's image on the head with an old key from his ancestral home—*le Bois Dormant*.

Le Pain dur seems to me a better play than *L'Otage*. History is here unobtrusive; the characters are far more clearly delineated than those of *L'Otage* and they have more life, particularly the women—Lumir and Sichel. Both are symbols of forces transcending the individual and also human time. The one, Sichel, a daughter of Israel, deeply aware of the age-old struggle of her people to regain a land of their own, realizes that at last, owing to the great upheaval of the French Revolution, the happiness of Israel may come here and now by mingling with other races, even at the cost of forsaking the ancient faith. The other, Lumir, soars upon the wings of an idealism which is of a purer kind, more uncompromising, more moving, more detached from the temporal, and is responsible for the finest poetry of the play. If Louis is without roots, Lumir is the living past, and the power of her character transfigures the scene where she reveals and arms this new Orestes. Even Louis can find moving accents of true poetry, and the passion which burns in Lumir inspires her with the kind of logic in which the terms of life and death have no meaning except as reference to the ' idea ' which guides her—the idea is Poland:

Il y a un sillage derrière moi que la mer ne suffit pas à disperser.
La Pologne, pour moi, c'est cette raie rose dans la neige, là-bas,
    pendant que nous fuyions,
Chassés de notre pays par un autre plus fort,
Cette raie dans la neige, éternellement!
J'étais toute petite alors, blottie dans les fourrures de mon père.
Et je me souviens aussi de cette réunion, la nuit, alors que la
    révolte commença.

(p. 359, vol. II)

Le Père Humilié

Act I. The first scene, with Sichel and her daughter Pensée, takes place at a masked ball in Rome. Pensée is dressed as Night, Sichel as Autumn. Pensée, who is blind, tells her mother of her love for Orian de Homodarmes, the Pope's nephew. The scene which follows as part of the exposition shows us Lady U. embodying the spirit of rising young Italy, Prince Wronsky as the Polish patriot dreaming of his oppressed country, and Coûfontaine as Napoléon III's ambassador in Rome, ready, as his father was, for any kind of compromise: *Mon nom est paix, accord, conciliation, transaction, entente, bonne volonté réciproque*, he says, not without irony. Scene III brings together the main protagonists of the drama—Pensée and Orian. They know that they belong to each other, that they were made for each other. Pensée says so explicitly at the end of the scene; she knows that Orian loves her and yet that he wishes to place between him and her an impassable barrier by marrying her to his brother, so that he himself may remain free to serve the Pope; nevertheless at the end of the scene the two lovers can no longer hide their feelings, and they confess their love for each other.

Act II. In the first scene we see the Pope, ' the humbled father ', as sad and as lonely as Christ on the last night in the olive groves. He is in such a state of dejection that a young monk has to console him. After that, his two nephews, Orian and Orso, come to ask his advice. Orso, who knows that his brother loves and is loved by Pensée, would like him to marry her. Orian would like his brother to marry Pensée, but he is no longer sure of his vocation. The Pope gives them his views on marriage:

> Mais le mariage n'est point le plaisir, c'est le sacrifice du plaisir, c'est l'étude de deux âmes qui pour toujours désormais et pour une fin hors d'elles-mêmes
> Auront à se contenter l'une de l'autre.
>
> (p. 439)

and continues by telling Orian that it is only by performing his earthly duty that he will reach God:

> Tu n'iras pas avec Dieu avant d'être débarrassé de ce que tu dois aux hommes.
> Orian, donne-leur la lumière! Il n'y a pas qu'une aveugle au monde.
>
> (p. 443 and variant)

[124]

and the Pope insists that Orian should do what he himself can no longer hope to do:

> Orian, mon fils, ce que je n'ai pu faire, fais-le, toi, qui n'as pas ce trône où je suis attaché pour mieux entendre le cri désespéré de toute la terre! ce supplice d'être attaché pendant que toute la terre souffre et qu'on sait qu'on a en soi le salut, toi qui n'as pas ce vêtement devant lequel, par la malice du diable, tous les coeurs reculent et se resserrent!
>
> (p. 444)

Act III. At the beginning of the Act Orso and Orian are alone, and Orso tells his brother that Pensée wishes to see him before they leave to join the French army engaged in defending Paris against the Prussians. Orian accepts, and to begin with he replies to Pensée in exactly the same terms as Prouhèze to Rodrigue:

> Quand je vivrai enfin, quand je ne serai plus cet Orian aveugle et à demi dormant, mais quelqu'un dans un rapport éternel enfin avec une cause raisonnable . . .
>
> (p. 457)

Orian has the same beliefs as Prouhèze: he believes that he can only belong to Pensée in God, yet he has agreed with what Pensée said to him before:

> Quand on vous préparait, Orian, je pense qu'il restait un peu de la substance qui avait été disposée en vous, et c'est de cela que vous manquez et que je fus faite.
>
> (p. 453)

In the end Orian gives in to Pensée's pleading, he remains with her in her darkness, and they belong to each other on earth, unmindful of God, who is excluded from their happiness. How can such a decision be explained? Perhaps because in the past:

> il y eut une femme jadis qui a sauvé le Pape,

a demoiselle de Coûfontaine, Pensée's ancestor, gave her life to save the Pope; now the Pope's nephew pays back the debt of his ancestor by breaking his vows and running thereby the risk of losing Heaven.

The question in this crucial scene is: will the lovers meet in Eternity or will they be excluded from God's Kingdom? We do not have to wait long for an answer. At the beginning of Act IV Orso comes to tell Pensée and her mother Sichel that Orian has been killed and that ' his soul is with God '. As for himself, he has come back to offer his name to Pensée so that the child born *d'une rencontre désespérée et sans aucune parole* may have a legal father, and he reassures Pensée by saying that *Celle qui fut à mon frère, croyez vous qu'elle soit jamais autre chose qu'une soeur pour moi?* So in the end Orian's and Pensée's love is accepted in God, while conventions and social laws are respected, so that love outside marriage finds its sanction both in God and in society.

Le Père Humilié is the weakest link of the trilogy. The atmosphere of far-fetched images which do not fit into the context, the heavy-footed fantasy, the bombast and cliché are never completely forgotten; how can one forget the clumsiness and lack of taste of such phrases as:

C'est orion qui est le danger pour Orian?

Puns of that degree of refinement are repeated more often than is necessary. Together with that, the love of the general, of the abstraction, that desire to widen the single person into something greater, such as a whole people or an historical movement, gives some of Claudel's heroes very shadowy figures and hollow voices. The central scene in *Le Père Humilié*, Scene II, Act III, where Pensée and Orian aim at a Corneillian grandeur, is merely unconvincing rhetoric. Deprived of that atmosphere of ineluctability which Claudel sought to infuse into the play, what seems like the sheer obstinacy of the heroes to act as symbols of historical movements or as instruments appointed by Providence for a definite task, destroys their individuality and makes their language sound as hollow as if it came from a mask. The symbolism is stretched to the point of unacceptability when Pensée says:

Il y eut une femme jadis qui a sauvé le Pape—un homme ne peut donner que sa vie, mais une femme peut donner plus encore—la mère de mon père, Sygne de Coûfontaine.
Et c'est sa fille maintenant sans yeux qui tend les mains vers celui que le Pape auprès de lui appelle son fils.

Et voici que dans mes veines le plus grand sacrifice en moi
s'est réuni à la plus grande infortune, et le plus grand orgueil,

Le plus grand orgueil à la plus grande déchéance et à la
privation de tout honneur, le Franc dans une seule personne
avec le Juif.

Tu es chrétien, et moi, ce qui coule dans mes veines, c'est le
sang même de Jésus-Christ, ce sang dont un Dieu fut fait,
maintenant dédaigné.

Pour que tu voies, c'est pour cela sans doute qu'il fallait que
je fusse aveugle.

Pour que tu aies la joie, il me fallait sans doute cette nuit
éternelle sans aucune parole que ma part est de dévorer!

(p. 454)

Pensée and Orian may see themselves as the respective symbols
of Israel and Christendom, but the reader is very remote from
such convictions, he has not been led to share the so-called
strong feeling which renders the earthly union of those forlorn
lovers impossible, the very feelings which are supposed to be the
motives of the dramatic tension and the source of his sympathy
for them. Just as he could not understand why Sygne had to
be sacrificed in order to save the Pope, in the same way now, he
cannot understand why Orian must sacrifice himself and Pensée's happiness in order to repay the Pope's debt and to save him.
One is left with the impression that Claudel's pious feelings
prevented him from realizing that neither the lives of the Popes
nor the lives of any other individuals, however much syn-
thesized and symbolized they may be, can impart to human
actions that power of inevitability which pervades Greek dramas and creates tension and pathos. One may add that when
the *dramatis personæ*, besides belonging to the Christian world,
belong not to the fabulous or legendary world but to history,
the only forces which may drive them on are those of the human
heart. That implies a power to scrutinize the psyche which
Racine possessed to a supreme degree, and which in our time
T. S. Eliot possesses to no mean degree, but which Claudel
certainly does not possess; for whatever qualities he has, he is
not a psychologist.

This trilogy, or this *Orestia*, as some critics like to call it, is
not to my mind a great achievement; the poetry is poor, and in
the case of *Le Père Humilié* the dramatic element is so weak as to

make the play not stage-worthy. While *L'Otage* is perhaps more dramatic if one can overcome the difficulties already discussed, the poetry is poorer than in *Le Pain dur*, which is perhaps the best poetic drama of the trilogy. Claudel has written other plays, such as *Protée, L'Ours et la Lune, La nuit de Noël*, etc., but none of them is on the level of those which we have examined, and none of them would, I think, contribute anything new to what has already been said about his poetic drama.

VIII

THEOLOGY AND LOVE IN CLAUDEL

CLAUDEL's conception of love is based on two assumptions which seem to defy logic. The first is that lovers who are made for each other, or who have in them the force and the truth which can enable them to reach the depths of each other's being and by so doing to reach the essence of being as God made it, will continue to love each other in Eternity and will live eternally in God. Claudel says so explicitly in *Le Soulier de Satin* :

> Maintenant je porte accusation contre cet homme et cette femme par qui j'ai existé une seconde seule pour ne plus finir et par qui j'ai été imprimée sur la page de l'éternité !
> Car ce qui a existé une fois fait partie pour toujours des archives indestructibles.
>
> (p. 952)

Such an assumption contains serious contradictions which we shall endeavour to examine later. For the moment let us retain only the most important, the one which forms the basis of the impossible dilemma in which Claudel has enclosed himself, a dilemma out of which he cannot escape without deserting the great principle which he seeks to glorify, for the predestination which is posited at the outset cannot be interrupted half-way in order to show that everything that happens is still *ad majorem dei gloriam*. The dilemma is that two people who are complementary and meant to love each other in God's Will nevertheless exclude God by the perfection of their love. Therefore their love, although God-made, cannot be.

The second assumption is that the woman, through her beauty, the image of eternal beauty, is the image of God. It is therefore through her (yet not in her) that man will reach God. Prouhèze, before she can hope to be Rodrigue's star, must renounce him completely on earth and in Heaven and bring her soul back to God in a state of absolute purity. Such a condition not only contradicts the metaphysical determinism posited about the origin of the two lovers and their faith that they will belong to each other in Eternity, but also introduces a strange separation between God and His creatures, a complete break between Time and Eternity; for it is only by returning to God in a state which will have retained absolutely nothing of their life in Time and beyond Time, since they were predestined to each other, that Prouhèze and Rodrigue will in a way be linked together in Eternity. There is no doubt that we are here faced with an unexplainable gap between Time and Eternity. Christ the Redeemer—God's expression and boundary in Time —is absent, and, without transition, we are asked to pass from the world of man to the world of God-Being and Non-Being, knowing all and yet not knowing—for He is without Christ, the mediator between creator and created, the means to return to Eternity and unknowing. If, as in Milton's words, ' *all things are of God* ', or as Blake said, ' *everything that lives is holy* ', everything that is had to be, could only be what it is, has always been so eternally in its essence and can neither be beyond God's Will —Christ—nor can return to God, except through Time. The world of Time is the world of Christ—God's word; and only things which have been created in Time through Christ, meeting point of Time and Eternity, can live in Eternity or in God, both the created and the uncreated, the total sum of Being and Non-Being.

If one accepts the premise that there may exist two beings God-created, meant to belong to each other, each having for the other something which only he or she has and will always have, one finds it difficult to understand how God could punish them for doing something they have been dedicated to. For Tristram there is, and there can only be, one Iseult, for Mésa there is only one Ysé, for Rodrigue there is only one Prouhèze, and all those lovers know that fact at once in a revelatory moment where Time and Eternity meet. If one of them has been allowed to marry the wrong partner, that surely can only be viewed as part of God's design, and therefore one cannot see any reasons why He should play such a game with His creatures, who, if they do what He meant them to do on earth, cannot but expect to be forgiven and to be reunited in Heaven, as is the case with the lovers in *Partage de Midi*. On the contrary, if, in spite of the fact that they have been created to love each other, they are condemned by God to eternal separation, as is the case with the lovers of *Le Soulier de Satin,* the arbitrariness of such tyrannical ways can only draw forth all our sympathy towards them. Besides that, we have here in this God-enforced separation an unthinkable suggestion of change in God's Will, a wilful transformation into nothingness of essences which were meant to create being. Of course only God could do that; yet, as such an operation implies fluctuations in the Eternal Will or, on the contrary, the existence of essences condemned to abortion, one would be compelled to accept the existence either of certain self-destructive forces extant in God Himself—a serious self-contradiction against the very principle of creation— or of certain possibilities of change of purpose which it would be difficult to accept as attributes of the Eternal Will.

The suggestion made by Claudel in the monologue of the moon—that spiritual union is something possible and which will grant the two partners Eternity—presupposes at least two pre- mises: the first that Eternity belongs only to the spirit and not to matter, and the second that evil can exist only in matter and not in the spirit. Such tenets are obviously very difficult to uphold either on theological or on philosophical grounds. The bodily assumption of Christ and of the Blessed Virgin, and the resurrection of the flesh on Judgment Day are arguments which militate strongly against a separation between body and spirit within the Christian doctrine. There is at this moment enough evidence to show that such an opposition between body and mind, matter and energy, is even more strongly resented in the new science and philosophy.

The belief that Eternal existence could be confined to Eternity to the exclusion of Time is even more arbitrary and more unacceptable. What is in Eternity is also in some ways in Time, for although Time may be only the shadow of the substance which is Eternity, the visible aspect of what is invisible, the being of the essence, the essence of Being in Time must be part of Eternity, and must needs have always existed in Eternity. What we call Time is in its essence as eternal as Eternity, since it is part of it. We call Time our apprehension of existence, which is only one of the modes of Being which is eternal. What we call Time is, therefore, always present, has always been and will always be; the only thing that seems to vary in a relative and limited way is the mode and intensity of the apprehension; but a thing can be apprehended only if it is; and if it is, or has been once, it is forever. If two people are complementary in their essences and necessary to each other in order to create Being, they must already have been so in Eternity, and the refusal to be in Time what they are meant to be from Eternity is a denial of what truly is, and an attempt to deny or to prevent (if the intervention were divine it would be self-contradictory) the eternal existence of a thing which by its essence is meant to be, and will only be eternally, once it has existed in Time. In that respect Time can be said to be the midwife of Eternity; nothing which has not truly existed in Time can be in Eternity (I mean by ' truly ' something which has reached the truth of the essence).

There are, of course, no definite ways or means of testing the absolute truthfulness of such moments when Eternity and Time meet. The saint who, like Joan of Arc, claims to hear God's voice, may well be credited with hearing ' daemonic ' voices and be treated accordingly by his fellow-beings. It is only when the saint's life has ended and he can be judged by his actions and their results, in brief by his existence, that we can attempt to find out and to describe what was the essence of his being. The only plane upon which such judgments can take place is the metaphysical, against the background of a complete acceptance of a belief in Transcendence which involves Life in Time and in Eternity. The saint takes certain decisions in the light of his absolute faith in God; some people may think that such a faith is only a projection of his ego, and not God's voice; yet if he is prepared to stake his life in Time and in Eternity upon his faith, surely nothing more can be said until one is in a position to see what has been his life's contribution to Mankind. If, for somebody who believes in Transcendence, final Truth does not come at the point of death—the point when the two sides of Life meet—one may wonder where else it could come. If a being believes, as he ought to, in the supreme goodness of God, he cannot believe that he has been created to go through Time with longings unsatisfied, with desperation in his heart, in order to reach or not to reach, as in *Le Soulier de Satin*, fulfilment in Eternity; for he knows that anything which has not been in Time will never be. Even God had to exist in Time in order to be all in one—the eternal possible, the supreme Being whose essence is to be Being, and also Non-Being.

Claudel's neatly compartmented theology enables him to carry out the demonstration he has set himself, and to escape at will from his *a priori* determinism. Prouhèze skilfully manages to meet God's requirements on all scores, and can use each of her assets—body and spirit—to take with it a human soul to Heaven. Born with Rodrigue's love in her heart, meant for him, she nevertheless marries, in God's Will, someone else. She can only have Rodrigue in Eternity by renouncing him on earth, yet she can also drag up to Eternity Don Camille, by yielding to him that body which she has refused to Rodrigue. Strange contortions, all God-made, all God-meant! Prouhèze is born for Rodrigue, but there is also in her something which has been made for Camille, as he himself explains to Prouhèze before Rodrigue comes to Mogador for his first and last interview with her. Camille is the instrument of Providence, he is bound to Prouhèze in the same way as Sygne is bound to Turelure, there is something in her soul which is necessary to his, which therefore belongs to his. The mask of evil which distorts Camille's face distorts ours also; we can see ourselves in him; we can see in him as in us the suffering God-Christ, waiting to be redeemed by the good which must prevail, and which must also be brought to Camille's soul. The good, the redeeming element in Camille's soul is its mysterious link with Prouhèze. There we have, in the microcosm of the soul, the epitome of the universe, good and evil existing in various degrees in everyone; the hangman's grin and the torturer's violence are also part of ourselves, of man who contains them all and also Christ—the suffering God who waits for the end of evil, which, in the absolute, can only be the end of creation.

Camille is a sinner, a sinner who, like Satan, has rebelled against God, and yet who believes in God, and who knows that Prouhèze is both the source of his rebelliousness and also of the Divine Grace which can save him. In order to bring him that Divine Grace she must belong wholly to God and to nobody else, not even to Rodrigue; in order to be the instrument created by Divine Providence to save the good—Rodrigue— and the bad—Camille—she must annihilate her human love completely and lay herself bare at the feet of her Maker. While Sygne was allowed to keep her heart for her cousin, Prouhèze is allowed no such compromise; with her the division between body and soul is no longer possible; she must renounce absolutely, in mind and body, in Time and Eternity, her love for Rodrigue if she wants to bring him back to God, which is something quite different from loving him in God. The compulsion placed upon her is more moving than that placed upon Sygne, because less arbitrary and involving feelings less repellent than those which are bound to occupy Sygne's heart at the thought of marrying her parents' murderer. The compulsion placed upon Prouhèze does not rest on any doubtful dogmatism, as might after all be the case with Badilon's beliefs; it rests on the very human plea of a man who believes and who knows that his salvation in Eternity depends on Prouhèze, who is asked to perform the highest act of Christian charity—the complete oblation of her soul in order to save another. There is no doubt that this final gesture of Prouhèze's is an attempt to unify Claudel's theology, yet he can do so only by wilfully breaking his self-imposed determinism which is the foundation of Prouhèze's and Rodrigue's love, therefore by showing God's decisions as being self-contradictory, and by making evil appear as part of God's responsibility. Making evil a necessity to the good renders evil meaningless, and as worthy of sympathy as any apparent good, since it is necessary to bring forth that good. In the end such a realization can only leave us with the pathos which arises from knowledge of the suffering and frustration of two good human beings who seem to be condemned by God to the terrible awareness of being meant to be one, and yet never being one, not even in Heaven; for Prouhèze must completely forsake her love for Rodrigue in order to be his star—something which he accepts, but which he certainly finds it difficult to understand.

The unavoidable inference which one is compelled to draw from Claudel's work is that God cannot accept the absolute happiness of two human beings on earth, because that complete happiness would exclude Him. Therefore although two beings may have been meant for each other in God's Will, they can be one outside marriage only in an incomplete way, with a wound which may inspire them with the constant desire to rise above their earthly condition towards their Maker. We have here assumptions which either destroy the *a priori* determinism or imply a wilfulness on the part of the Divinity to display a strange casuistry of intention. If neither of these interpretations is valid, one can only say that one is faced with a contradiction of language impossible to understand. In *Partage de Midi* the two lovers, Ysé and Mésa, yield to the force of their predestined love with the knowledge of their failing, yet trusting in God's forgiveness. How their love can be both predestined and yet in some ways a sin against God is difficult to see. In *Le Père Humilié* the Pope attempts to discriminate, without success, between his nephew's love of Pensée and marriage; the two lovers do not marry, but they have a child together, and we are explicitly told that Orian, after his death, has gone to Heaven. In *Le Soulier de Satin* the consummation of love is avoided through circumstances independent of the lovers. Prouhèze's guardian angel has to be constantly by her side to prevent her from doing what Ysé could not help doing in the faith that her love was meant for Eternity.

With the exception of Dona Musique and the Viceroy of Naples—a couple of very insignificant lovers—marriage in Claudel's plays is either a deterrent to adultery or merely a loveless business arrangement—Sygne and Turelure, Sichel and Turelure's son, Prouhèze and Camille, Pensée and Orso, etc. The true lovers do not marry, even when they have the possibility of doing so. After the death of her husband, Prouhèze could have married Rodrigue, yet she marries Camille. Jacques Hury does not marry Violaine; he marries Mara. The true lover, like the great mystics, craves for absolute union with the beloved being. Such a union can be achieved only through great intensity and under the stimulus of an overwhelming anxiety to reach the source of love. This conception of love, which runs parallel to the love of the unattainable and the unachieved of the Romantics, is in Claudel something similar to Pascalian despair or Kierkegaardian *Angst,* and becomes the basis of the search for and the knowledge of God. It is only by loving without complete satisfaction and in despair that the lovers discover one another's true identity, which is in God. The woman being only the image of God, the shadow of the substance can never satisfy man completely, but she can awaken him to and bring him to Eternity. Thence the idea which prevails in Claudel, that the woman is only the instrument meant to carry out God's purpose, the means to inflict upon man the wound which will awaken him to his true nature. Therefore Claudel's women are beautiful but unstable—at least, they give their lovers the impression of being unstable and of having betrayed them. Such are Lala, Léchy, Ysé; and even the purest, Prouhèze and Violaine, give their lovers the impression that they have been unfaithful to them. If the lovers reached complete satisfaction, they would form a closed whole from which God would be excluded, therefore absolute love cannot be found in marriage. The elect, the few who, like Violaine, are born with passionate natures capable of experiencing the supreme intensity of love, a love which is in a way supra-human, find it impossible to compromise; their love must be everything. In *La jeune fille Violaine*, second version, Pierre de Craon, who knows that Violaine is already chosen by God, explains to her that there is a love which transcends the human, and yet which may embrace it too, but from that play onwards these two aspects of love are completely separate in Claudel's theatre, and Pierre de Craon's speech does not appear in *L'Annonce faite à Marie*.

Absolute love in Claudel is not possible on earth and can be reached only beyond the earth and marriage, in God. The only marriage which Claudel allows between his true lovers is the non-sacramental marriage between souls meant to belong to each other for all time. At the end of *Partage de Midi* Ysé and Mésa consent to each other. When one of those perfect lovers is compelled to marry somebody who is not the truly loved one, he gives that partner only the body but not the soul. Prouhèze marries Camille, but her soul belongs to Rodrigue, and her child, as if to show the miraculous influence of soul upon body, resembles the latter. Jacques Hury marries Mara, but again when their son is resurrected by Violaine his eyes become the same colour as those of Violaine, and spiritually he is her son, and not Mara's. Sygne marries Turelure, but keeps her heart for her cousin, and Pensée marries Orso, but only on condition that he renounces all his conjugal rights. Two lovers destined to each other cannot belong to anybody else. In *Le Soulier de Satin* the dying Jesuit refers to ' the imperishable kinship ' which exists between the essences of Rodrigue and Prouhèze: *L'intégrité primitive et leur essence même telle que Dieu les a conçus autrefois dans un rapport inextinguible !* and the angel himself acknowledges the righteousness of Prouhèze's view; when she says that she existed only through Rodrigue, he says: *C'est en lui que tu étais nécessaire.* It is in Rodrigue that lies her necessity—it is of course the eternal Rodrigue which both the angel and Prouhèze are referring to.

But then two questions arise here in connection with this concept. The first one is a simple one and concerns the problem of free-will; it is at once clear that if a man and a woman are predestined to each other there is no freedom of choice; in order to get out of that difficulty, Claudel seems to accept a certain amount of trial and error on earth; but whatever they may do, in the end he brings his lovers together in Eternity. The second one involves him in contradictions and insuperable difficulties. In spite of the fact that Rodrigue's and Prouhèze's promises have been described as indissoluble, Prouhèze asks Rodrigue to release her from her promise; now this is something which obviously goes beyond them both, since they are predestined for each other. Yet another point is that one cannot see how there will be any possibility of meeting between Prouhèze and Rodrigue in Eternity, since Prouhèze has to return to God a soul which must be completely free of any earthly memories, a soul which will be merged into the great one which will also contain Rodrigue's. In the end it does look as if Rodrigue had been visited by a strange vision which spurred him to action on earth but which will never, not even in Eternity, quench the frustration with which he is left and which he accepts as being within God's Will.

Up to *Le Soulier de Satin* Claudel's lovers were reconciled in Eternity, and enjoyed from then on eternal bliss. Such is, in spite of all the wreckages strewn in their human path, the end of

Partage de Midi when Ysé says that she has nothing to wait for:
Plus rien que l'amour à jamais, plus rien que l'éternité avec toi!
Jacques Hury lives and will die with Violaine's presence in his
soul, and Violaine, although very saintly—even a saint,
perhaps—is not God: at the very point of death she has not
renounced her love for Jacques Hury, and that love, in spite of
her spiritual vocation, or perhaps as part of her spiritual vocation, is also part of her and seems destined to continue in Eternity. Orian dies having sinned against the laws of the Church,
yet he is with God, as his brother Orso says. In *Le Soulier de
Satin* Claudel sought to reconcile two irreconcilable concepts of
love—that of the predestined couple of lovers who will love each
other in life and beyond death into Eternity in God's presence,
and that which consists in using one of the lovers, the woman,
as a lure for the great love of God, Who places in man's mind
illusions of perenniality, and flashes a woman's face across his
eyes in order to lead him back to His sacred Kingdom. By so
doing Claudel involves God in contradictions and in an
arbitrariness of behaviour which may in the end lead the humble
human creature to murmur with Vigny that perhaps: *Seul le
silence est grand, tout le reste est faiblesse.*

CLAUDEL AS A POET

POETIC drama is a social art, and as such has to reckon with its audience, whose taste and responses are continually changing. The language of poetic drama can oscillate between the directness and clarity of that of Racine, and Shakespeare's unique combination of precision and wealth, but either language must have the external appearance of a common norm generally accepted by the age which uses it. The alexandrine was the norm of Racine's age, just as the blank verse was the norm of Shakespeare's age. In Racine the words are simple, as in Dante; the poetry is direct and expresses moments of very great intensity in what seems sometimes to be rather flat language without images or metaphors, or with images which are very simple and drawn from everyday life. In Shakespeare the poetry is more complex, very often indirect, and with flights into realms where the mind and heart are lit by a turmoil of falling stars, images, and metaphors of unfathomable depth. In both cases we have revelatory poetry, poetry which, starting from the object whence it rises, gives the work of art an aura of transcendence which poetry alone can supply.[1]

It seems to me that if the poet has to-day to try to compete with the novel and the cinema, he will have to do so on their own ground, that is, by using themes and a language which can

---

[1] True poetry, even merely descriptive poetry, is revelatory; starting from the phenomenon, it rises towards the ' noumenon '. The poetry of Dante was consciously symbolical; the scientific spirit of the Renaissance did not become part of Western man's consciousness until Descartes; through the sixteenth and the greater part of the seventeenth century the sense of the numinous, the belief in transcendence, remained as the epiphenomenon of an increasingly objective phenomenalism. With Romanticism in England, and Symbolism in France, we return to poetry as conscious revelation through imagination. The words of Shelley 'Poetry lifts the veil from the hidden beauty of the world, and makes familiar objects be as if they were not familiar ', are echoed by Baudelaire's attempts *de s'emparer d'un paradis révélé*, and by Rimbaud's aim of *se faire voyant*.

rub their skins against the bare, direct dialogue of the novel, the speech form of the cinema or that of the plain man in the street. Yet at the same time it must be a language suffused with strength and rhythm which can at any given moment by a heightening of tension, a powerful image or a metaphor, be transubstantiated into the language of true poetry. This is the language of Eliot, in *The Cocktail Party*, but on the whole, not that of Claudel, for his is packed with images and metaphors which, though of a supreme value in poetry, have only a rather relative value in the drama of an age dominated by prose; of course this does not mean that there may not come a time when Claudel's prodigality and richness will be appreciated by a generation who have passed from poetic-convalescence to full health. Above all it does not mean that the convalescent diet should be maintained too long, or that the shock treatment applied by Claudel is valueless or æsthetically unsound if one accepts the vital distinction between drama and tragedy towards which, on the whole, Claudel tends. It is true that his characters are all in God's hands, but the same is true of *Athalie*, probably the closest approximation to Greek tragedy that Christian civilization has produced. The Christian God, ' the God of the Jews ' is as compelling in this play as the inexorable fate which pursues Œdipus or the Atrides. Ineluctable compulsion—internal or external, God-willed or self-made, yet just as unexplainable and as unavoidable as in the case of *Lear*—is the foundation of tragedy. These considerations suggest a brief mention of two points about which I am not quite at one with Mr. Eliot's views. I hasten to say that it is something which could probably be cleared up by an elaboration of meaning which Mr. Eliot has not attempted, or by the mere repudiation of any finality about a problem which he himself still professes to be investigating.

First, the problem of verse and prose in poetic drama. I fully agree with all he says about the advantages of poetry over prose and the necessity of verse in poetic drama; I agree that the verse rhythm has a subconscious effect which prepares hearers for the moments of ' intensity ', yet I cannot help feeling that such an advantage can easily be offset by a too obvious artificiality of the verse. The argument that if a play contains both poetry and prose, the audience is conscious of the transitions, and is therefore inclined to suspect the poetry of artificiality, does not seem to me to be well-founded. Every emotion has its own rhythm and its special mode of expression. If one tries to impose a verse pattern on something which has no emotional background but is merely communication at a very superficial level, one introduces a form of artificiality more serious than the ' possible ' artificiality of poetry side by side with prose. It seems to me that a mere uniformized and, at certain points, externally imposed form is far more dangerous and liable to sound artificial in serious plays (and ' serious ' is the key-word) than a mixture of prose and poetry. There is no fundamental difference between the two: the difference is merely a difference of intensity of feelings (including thought) which imposes a metrical rhythm which lasts as long as the emotion lasts; once the emotion subsides, it is natural to revert to the freedom of rhythm without definite metre which is prose. The stronger the emotion, the more definite and sustained the metrical rhythm, the emotion being sometimes so actual and so strong that it is beyond words and can be conveyed only by very elemental, yet essential, rhythm. But it seems to me that in serious plays rhythm should be free to vary according to the need of the emotion to which it organically corresponds, and not be subjected to a fixed metrical pattern which can only be at times artificial. This surely is the trouble with opera. It sounds natural to sing *Lucevano le stelle* or for that matter ' My love is like a red, red rose ', but it would be incongruous to sing ' Oh my dear, pass me the salt '. Indeed, in an age when prose is the normal literary medium, verse is apt to sound artificial, unless it is informed with the emotive intensity which lifts its pattern into poetry.

The second point I wish to mention is directly connected with the first, and is an elaboration of a passing remark which Mr. Eliot makes at the end of his lecture on ' Poetry and Drama ',[1] where, after having praised Ibsen and Chekhov, he suggests ' that they may have been hampered in expression by writing prose. This peculiar range of sensibility can be expressed by dramatic poetry at its moments of greatest

[1] T. S. Eliot, *Selected Prose*, Penguin Books, 1953, p. 85.

[141]

intensity. At such moments we touch the border of those feelings which only music can express '. This is the Wagnerian theory, the theory which implies that there are feelings and emotive states beyond the realm of words, feelings which can only be suggested by music which, in contradistinction to poetry, is a ' vague ' art. This was the cardinal belief of the ' symbolist school ' of poetry, yet not of Mallarmé, who knew better than any of them, who outlined very clearly the distinction between heard and unheard music, and who maintained the supremacy of the word over music—heard music, of course: *La poésie proche l'idée, est Musique par excellence—ne consent pas d'infériorité.*[1] Mallarmé's journey was that of Beethoven in the Ninth Symphony, from music to the words, and for Mallarmé, from the contingent to the essence. In the balcony scene of *Romeo and Juliet*—the example quoted by Mr. Eliot to show his ' mirage of verse drama which presents at once the two aspects of dramatic and musical order '—the poetry is song, the revelation of two enchanted souls filled with the sublime passion which makes heavenly joy: the substance not so much of Wagner's as of Mozart's music, which is, above all, joy. In Wagner, music takes over where words leave off, in order to express emotions which overflow them. To be precise, this music tries to express not so much the depths or the heights of the human soul as an *excess* of feelings over words and means of verbal expression, a longing for something indefinable, the something which has been so widely felt and misinterpreted by the romantics. But, *excess* of feelings does not necessarily imply depth or supra-human sensibility: it may only imply the lack of the necessary genius to coalesce these feelings into form, for, paraphrasing Coleridge, we might say that no truly *essential* feeling or thought can lack its form without, by so doing, denying its very existence. This, then, is not music tending towards the Essence or the Idea—the pure music of Plato, source of all things—but music as a vague art. It is not music as an ontological means of expressing or conveying the essential truth, but music designed to convey the state of turgidity and indefinable agitation which hides the great calm and the perennial quality of the depths. We are

---

[1] Mallarmé, *Oeuvres Complètes*, Gallimard, p. 381.

left half-way in a vagueness favourable to relative subjectivity
and apt to satisfy the creative itch of the masses, but incom-
patible with the pursuits of the mind interested in the Goethean
journey towards ' greater and greater light '. I do not mean
that great art reveals and solves all mystery, for mystery is
part of great art, and Goethe's urge was perhaps too strong
in that direction. I mean rather that in great art the phenomenal world, the world of the senses, which is our only means of
apprehending the essence, must be clearly outlined and clearly
conveyed, whether through words, pigments, lines, or notes,
in images, objects, symbols, and sensations which have both
interaction and suggestiveness, but are not themselves vague.
Reality, in order to be transcended into its timelessness, must
not be wrapped up in a haze or drowned in vague sounds, but
clearly outlined, so that it may radiate clearly towards the sun
which we cannot see, but which gives it life. Vagueness can
suggest emotive states favourable to dreams or phantasmagoria,
but cannot provoke experiences informed by truth. That Mr.
Eliot is well aware of these implications is fully borne out by
the following statement: ' Some writers appear to believe that
emotions gain in intensity through being inarticulate. Perhaps
the emotions are not significant enough to endure daylight.' [1]
In the balcony scene of *Romeo and Juliet* the words are not a
means of suggesting by their music or rhythm something
impossible to say, as is often the case with Wagner, whose
music is very didactic and rhetorical. The words are the very
thing itself, they are nothing else but themselves—a song of
joy, like so much of Mozart's music, the pure elation of revealed
love—they are as complete in their plenitude as the end of the
Choral Symphony, which moves from music and vagueness
towards the perfection and purity of the words; and in both
cases the words are informed by an intensity of passion.

Poetry depends a good deal on music, the music of sounds
and rhythm; but poetry in moments of intensity tends towards the very essence of things. That essence is also their
structural rhythm, the Idea of Plato, the unheard music,
inaudible except in moments of strange ecstasy whose recollection can only hint at the real experience; something so remote

[1] *The Sacred Wood*, Methuen, 1920, p. 84.

from the music of the senses as to have nothing in common with it, except the analogical resemblances of fluidity. By comparison, the fluidity of the heard music is imprecision of feeling, obtained through precision of composition. The other kind of fluidity is fixed fluidity; it is the fluidity of the idea, ever changing in its search for form, ever the same at its source, and finally, of course, the same in its perennial form—the true form which expresses the essence. This type of poetry has nothing much to do with drama, though it has plenty to do with tragedy, which rests more on states of sensibility and feelings born from actions whose mainsprings are beyond the protagonists' control, than on drama, which is action. The other type of poetry, the type which makes use of heard music, also has plenty to do with drama, but here again mostly with drama which is serious and in which the action overflows into states of sensibility in which the poetry is revelatory of these states and not, on the whole, preparatory and ancillary to action. It is a poetry which, since it does not generally lead up to, or will action, takes over from rhetoric and is rooted less in the conscious than in the subconscious. In the difference between these two types of poetry lies the main difference between drama and tragedy, a difference which carries with it the inference that drama can stand only a certain limited type of poetry, while the greater, the more universal form of poetry pertains to tragedy. All that Valéry could remember of *Phèdre* was ' a succession of lyrical moments '. For Yeats, ' tragic art, passionate art, the drowner of dykes, the confounder of understanding, moves us by setting us to reverie, by alluring us almost to a state of trance '.

X

CLAUDEL'S ART POETIQUE

CLAUDEL began to write in an age when certain forms of literary expression were once more called into question. The second half of the nineteenth century was the age of scientific discoveries, industrial progress, and profound belief in reason and scientific methods. By the middle of the nineteenth century people were tired of the exuberance and of the much-heralded individualism of the Romantics, and they were ready to welcome the application of scientific methods of control and close observation of facts to the arts. So we had the Parnassian, the lover of impassive beauty, and the Realist, who, like Zola, could apply to art the same clinical detachment and keen observation of facts which characterize the scientist at work in his laboratory. But in art as well as in life there are no complete divisions into black and white; the various genres whose separation is strongly stressed in texts of literary analysis intermingle and overlap continuously in life, and strange as it may seem, Victor Hugo, Heredia, Zola, Rimbaud, and Baude-laire were contemporaries. Yet literary criticism gives each one, and with a wide enough amount of truth, different labels— Victor Hugo is labelled a romantic, Heredia a parnassian, Zola a realist, Rimbaud and Baudelaire symbolists; one could add Flaubert, who is generally described both as a realist and as a romantic; one can see at once the insuperable difficulties which arise when juggling with labels and when trying to affix them to something as complex as life or its expression—art. Each one of these descriptive words has a residuum of truth which compels a quasi-general acceptance, yet we cannot but find ourselves on the verge of untruth if we try to force upon them very definite categorical meanings which are valueless without the context of history. All the various meanings of these words can easily be present in the same man; it is only a matter of degree. Baudelaire, for instance, could rightly stand all those epithets in turn, in a way which proves the co-existence of all those attributes of art in the same man, yet he is described, and with sound reasons, as a symbolist.

Symbolism is not new, it is at least as old as literary expression; it ranges from the apocalyptic symbolism of the Bible to the crystalline, sparingly used symbols of the classical age; it is part of the process of conveying suggestions of a sometimes unapprehensible reality, yet a reality which is neither accepted as being nothing but rational nor beyond the final grasp of the conscious. But if we mean by symbolism a new way of conveying through the arts experiences of inner and outer reality, a conscious attempt not to describe what cannot be described, but rather to convey the totality of an experience which fuses subject and object, something which involves the whole being in a timeless moment and implies a new attitude to language, then symbolism began with Baudelaire and Rimbaud and soon became the self-conscious artistic creed which since the 1880's has dominated modern art. Whether they were described as classic, romantic, parnassian, or realist, all the writers who come under these headings had on the whole been concerned with describing reality, physical or psychical, in clear, rather representational, language. None of them could be labelled obscure. The symbolists proclaimed their desire to remain faithful to reality, but took different roads. They felt, with Baudelaire and Rimbaud, that reality was so complex, so intricately interwoven with the world of mind and imagination, that it could no longer be described, but merely hinted at, suggested through means which would enable the reader, the listener, or the spectator to recapture the image of that reality. That was symbolism in literature, and impressionism in music and painting—both in a way refinements of realism in the arts.

By the end of the eighteenth century, the importance of the mystery and the impenetrability of its core had come to light through the great mind of Kant who showed the limitations of Cartesianism and the fact that man's sensorial apparatus could only apprehend the phenomenon but not the 'noumenon', which could only be hinted at, apprehended intuitively through imagination. That was the attitude which underlay in various degrees the whole of the English romantic movement from Blake to Shelley; in France there was Rousseau, but we had to wait till the symbolists, Rimbaud and Baudelaire, for its complete emergence.

In France by the end of the nineteenth century artists and thinkers realized that the attempt to seize reality in its essence and to fix it in artistic creations was vain. They realized that the noumenon eluded the grasp of the mind compelled to content itself with the phenomenon, for in the end pure thought is non-thought, the mystical experience of the void, an experience which can only be mnemonic, secondary not primary, phenomenological and not ontological. In the end they came to realize that the only reality which man can grasp is not that of the external world subject to scientific laws, but that which lies in man's consciousness of that external world and in psychological time, the meeting point of being and non-being, the ever-moving present. The long descriptions of Flaubert or of Balzac limited reality, deformed it in the same way as Corbet or Millet limited it with their solid lines and their ethical connotations. The exact word, the precise image, the clear-cut line, killed true reality, and put in its place a picture of it reduced to proportions which everybody could apprehend. Symbolists and impressionists retained their sense of mystery towards reality, and they realized that they could convey an impression of that reality only with colours or sensuous words or images brought together according to psychological affinities, and not according to the logical laws of language or of factual observation. So, with them, we enter a period of coloured phenomenalism and musical and pictorial impressions of the words in an art in which the eyes and the mind, deprived of concrete lines and points to hold on to, rose steadily like the flames of fire to fade away into the ecstasy of the atmosphere or the void which surrounds them. That was the Mallarméan journey.

Claudel is a man of his age, the age of Symbolism, the age of Baudelaire and of Mallarmé, and above all of Rimbaud, who has been, according to Claudel himself, the greatest influence of his life: ' It is to Rimbaud ', said Claudel, ' that on the human plane I owe my return to faith. . . . The first glimmer of the truth came to me with the works of that great poet Arthur Rimbaud, to whom I owe eternal gratitude (and he has had a predominant influence on the formation of my thought). Whoever has been caught once under the spell of Rimbaud, is from then on as incapable of freeing himself from it as from the spell of the music of Wagner.' [1] Rimbaud never ceased to exercise a strange fascination on Claudel, who says at the end of his preface to the works of Rimbaud published by the Mercure de France: ' I am one of those who believe in his words, one of those who have had faith in him.' It was Rimbaud who more than anybody else was responsible for the changes in poetic diction which were later to be co-ordinated and expounded as the doctrine of the new school of poetry. Free verse, the use of assonances instead of rhyme, and the full development of a prose fluid, lyrical, moulded on the rhythm of hallucinatory visions and breath-taking emotions, will always remain associated with his name; above all, the pre-dominance of the symbol and of the image in poetry dates from Rimbaud. In *Une Saison en Enfer, Alchimie du verbe*, Rimbaud has tried to explain the method of his new art, and how he invented the colour of vowels, and tried to create a poetic speech which would be accessible to all the senses. Rimbaud was the seer, the prophet searching for the rediscovery of the formula which would enable him to contemplate again the lost Eden and to recover the primitive state of ' son of the sun '. He it was who could see a mosque in the sky instead of a factory, he it was who believed that words surging from the mysterious unconscious could reveal the true existence of things, and he it was who believed that in certain states of hallucination or self-hypnosis the two terms of a metaphor acquired the same reality, and the image and the thing imaged were one and the same thing. For him the word which came to him in that state was the key to the hidden world, and the poet in the moment of creation repeated God's creation when He named all things to the first man.

There is no need to point out the numerous similarities of belief which exist between Rimbaud and Claudel. Just as

---

[1] ' Arthur Rimbaud ', *Nlle. Revue Française*, 1st October, 1912, p. 563.

Claudel refused to accept the orthodox forms of drama and chose to concern himself with the exteriorization of his inner truth in his own personal way, in the same way he refused to comply with the accepted canons of poetic diction. He may, of course, have been influenced by the ideas and beliefs of his age, although it may be truer to say that he was part of his age and one of the chosen few through whom those beliefs could come to consciousness; he expresses his age, and, by individuating its most advanced forces, he apparently detaches himself from it. Claudel, like Rimbaud, represents that aspect of knowledge predominant at the end of the nineteenth century and to a certain extent in our time, which accepts the indissoluble relationship between subject and object and places knowledge at the point where they become one in a language which then acquires an ontological force transcending time. For Claudel the poetic genius must be more concerned with trying to grasp at once as many signs as possible of the revelation which comes to him, rather than with trying to order it into a form which will be readily apprehensible to all. He is not concerned with the reader, he is primarily concerned with his mission as a poet, which is to listen to those mysterious revelatory voices, to see the visions and to transcribe them into words at once, as quickly and as completely as possible. Hence like Rimbaud his use of concentrated symbols and images which he refuses to unravel: *Je suis un peu ivre en sorte qu'un autre mot parfois vient à la place du vrai,* he says, but what does it matter? Why worry with the reader? ' O reader, patient pathfinder on elusive tracks, the author who led you here handling his arguments in the same way as Calus dealt with stolen cattle . . . wishes you well! As for me, my hands freed, I take up again pipe and drum and I shut behind me the door of the Lodge of Medicine '.[1]

For Claudel the poet is the one who brings to life the whole of creation and God in the middle of it, since God made it and holds it together. ' The true poet ' says Claudel, ' is not the one who invents but the one who brings things together and by so doing enables us to understand them '.

---

[1] *Art Poétique,* p. 743.

Mon désir est d'être le rassembleur de la terre de Dieu!
Comme Christophe Colomb quand il mit à la voile,
    Sa pensée n'était pas de trouver une terre nouvelle,
    Mais dans ce coeur plein de sagesse la passion de la limite et
de la sphère calculée de parfaire l'éternel horizon.[1]

In his study of Dante, Claudel says that ' the object of
poetry is not as it is so often said, dreams, illusions and ideas,
but that holy reality given once and for all, and at whose
centre we are placed. It is the universe of visible things to
which Faith adds that of invisible things. All that is God's
creation which is the inexhaustible source of the narrations and
songs of the greatest poets as of the smallest of birds. . . . One
of the essential traits of great poetry is its catholicity . . . I
mean to say that the foremost poets have received from God
such vast things to express that the whole world is necessary
to their task.' [2] We can see how, in this finite world submitted
to God's order, man neither needs to yield to Pascalian despair
at the thought of his finitude in the infinite universe, nor adopt
the fierce individualism of the Romantics and their faith in
the immanence of Nature in a world without transcendence, or
rather in a world in which man and Nature have assumed
God's transcendence. In the world of Claudel transcendence
belongs exclusively to God, and immanence, which is inherent
to creation, can be felt by man's consciousness through Divine
Grace in moments when man reaches beyond himself towards
the eternal reality.

Claudel's religious and poetic beliefs are firm and precise,
and they place the poet within a reality which gives his work a
consistency, a precision of line which ought to exclude anarchy
and shapelessness completely. Yet, as we have seen, he is very
far from having avoided these feelings, and in fact most of them
flow directly from the beliefs which he holds, for a man who
believes that the poet's task is to express God's creation, and
that he does so under God's inspiration, will necessarily have
little patience with the impediments which tend to hold back
the powerful utterances which seek life through him. In his
desire to express to the full those forces which are in him,
Claudel puts his complete trust in inspiration, and inspiration

[1] La Maison Fermée, *Cinq Grandes Odes*, p. 160.   [2] *Art Poétique*, p. 793.

cannot be fettered by rules. In an interview published by F. Lefèvre in *Les Nouvelles Littéraires* in April 1925, Claudel says that it has been for him a true joy and a great relief to keep as far as possible away from classical models. He not only shares Victor Hugo's rebellious spirit against Classical dramaturgy, but he goes much further; *Le Soulier de Satin* is more vast, more complex than any drama of Victor Hugo's. The latter did not have as a driving force the anarchic spirit of Rimbaud; he still believed in the unity of action, in grammar, in certain rules of diction, and in the beauty of regular verse. Claudel has no such inhibitions. 'The greatest writers have never been able to accept laws made by grammarians, but they have sought to improve them, and not only by their will, but by their whims ',[1] and Renan, Taine, Voltaire, and other molochs of the eighteenth century are dismissed with utter contempt.

As we have seen in the course of our examination of his drama, Claudel does not aim at conveying character and action according to the normal rules of logical development. Speech, which is the medium by which character and action are revealed, is therefore not analytical but synthetic. 'Objects and their relationships ', Claudel says, ' do not strike our minds as separate things but as masses or conglomerates. Poetry, which aims at bringing them to life, will henceforth be a synthesis of ideas and images neither disconnected nor analysed, nor arranged in logical order, but presented in their original living state.'[2] As these thoughts and feelings group themselves according to the rhythm of the emotion which underlies them, the line should show the pattern of that emotion, and the blanks in the page are as important as the words themselves.

> O mon âme! le poème n'est point fait de ces lettres que je plante comme des clous, mais du blanc qui reste sur le papier.
> O mon âme, il ne faut concerter aucun plan! ô mon âme sauvage, il faut nous tenir libres et prêts,
> Comme les immenses bandes fragiles d'hirondelles quand sans voix retentit l'appel automnal![3]

The blanks must be filled by the reader's efforts. Claudel's phrase does not follow a normal, logical progression; it jumps

[1] *Réflexions*, II, p. 570. [2] *Réflexions*, I, pp. 417–19. [3] *Les Muses*, p. 17.

from one object, one image, to another, neglecting grammatical transitions. But the lack of logical sequence is only apparent, for Claudel's poetry has always some central image or symbol which links the whole thing together, and gives it imaginative oneness. Claudel never aims at describing or analysing, but always at making us share with him the coming to consciousness of certain emotions and ideas. The poet and the reader know together.

In that respect he is to a large extent operating against the genius of the French language, which is precise, analytical, descriptive, and does not lend itself readily to suggestiveness and imprecision. But genius can create both the form through which the substance which is in himself will find expression, and the public taste to make that form and substance acceptable. As far as form is concerned, Claudel is not entirely on new ground; he continues and develops in his own original way the experiments of Rimbaud, and the ' free verse ' of the symbolists. Like Rimbaud, Claudel believes in the revelatory power of the word; for Rimbaud the words were the cabalistic signs of hidden reality, for Claudel they are the key to the great mystery of creation centred on God. For Mallarmé the words are everything; they are transcendence in themselves, and the universe exists in order to be embodied in a great book which Mallarmé, high priest of this new art, always hoped to write. The only transcendence which Mallarmé accepts is that of art, which became for him the supreme end of Life. Like many poets, Claudel has tried to define his poetry and to theorize about it. In order to do so he presents us with a very personal distinction between prose and poetry. Prose for him ' is only concerned with knowing, with giving an exact, complete analytic description of things. Poetry's aim is to give æsthetic pleasure.' [1] We shall not reopen the much-debated theme of prose and poetry; we shall limit ourselves to a few remarks about Claudel's views and their influence on his work.

Few, very few poets would accept his definition of poetry; in fact, he himself does not, since he explains that the poet's task is to reveal the truth of God's creation; he does it in a work of art whose æsthetic perfection implies truth, but his

[1] *Réflexions*, I, p. 418.

search, as Wordsworth pointed out, is for truth. Wordsworth of course did not see any fundamental difference between poetry and prose; neither did Shelley, for that matter. Yet Shelley would not have subscribed to Wordsworth's view that the only difference between poetry and prose is metre, and that everything that can be said in poetry can be said in prose—or perhaps he might, if the operative word were ' said '. For although a great deal of poetry is like prose, concerned with saying, with describing thoughts and feelings, it is perhaps more true to say that poetry and what is sometimes called poetic prose are concerned with conveying experiences and with a search for a kind of knowledge which cannot be approached in any other way, for lying as it does beyond sense observation and analytical exploration, it can only be hinted at, glanced at in moments when the whole being is involved in that search or in the reception of the result of that search. Such moments are found in Rousseau and in Bossuet, when the division between the conscious mind and the object examined ceases, and when they both merge into the oneness of language, which in these rare timeless moments is all. We can indeed easily see that there is no essential difference between poetry and prose, the language used being the same, the difference being in the creative process which in poetry confers upon the word an ontological power, while in normal prose the word remains the instrument used to achieve a given end. Still, it may be wise not to lose sight of the fact that, although the words used in poetry and prose are the same, poetry fundamentally is the expression of powerful feelings felt on extraordinary occasions, and although prose may encounter such occasions, it deals more with the purely logical aspects of human life, and it is used to deal with themes which are beyond the normal scope of poetry because their nature is such that they can only be dealt with adequately in prose, whose primary aim is to convey the maximum of clarity in meaning. The supreme power of the poet is imagination; the supreme power of the prose writer is reason.

Poetry in a play is not stage directions; it is there to be spoken as the poet's experience suggested it. What, above all, counts in poetic drama is the performance, the saying of the words, and not the action. If Shakespeare had wanted the battle of

Actium to be mimed, he would not have described it lengthily, so that it might be lived through words; he would merely have given stage directions. If, in the first meeting of Romeo and Juliet, action had been the thing that mattered, he would hardly have felt the need to present the whole episode in sonnet form. Probably the best way to stress this point is by using the analogy of opera, an art in which it is not the physical action that is of supreme importance, but, on the contrary, the singing and the music which portray the action, in a way similar to that of the poet who portrays it with words which are not meant to be mere indications for realistic representation, but the means to suggest to the reader or listener complex experiences imaginatively lived. The question of poetry or prose is not a matter of choice, but of necessity. The writer who deals with an experience in prose does so because he feels it and lives it in prose—that is to say, he lives it at a level different from the level of the life of poetry. It is by no means a matter of conscious decision; it depends above all on the way a person is made. Obviously, if an experience comes to someone, or rather is lived by someone, at the depths where poetry takes place—which means at the most profound and complex imaginative depths where images, metaphors, and rhythms are integral parts of the life of the subject—it will *ipso facto* be poetry, of a kind, of course, and not prose. It is not at all a matter of choice at will; one cannot decide in advance on the form that an experience will have; it all depends on the type of experience and on the subject who lives it; and if one chooses or decides in advance what form an experience should have (and an experience once begun may be such as to break the conscious boundaries which one seeks to impose upon it), the choice is between describing and analysing something which has already a conceptual outline—prose, and living something one comes to know while it unfolds itself—which is some kind of poetry. Indeed, the poetic journey is not an attempt to clothe ideas in words, images, or symbols which will illustrate and explain them, it is not a progression towards a given end carried out through the logical relations of the words, a progression which, starting from experience, leaves it behind as a snake leaves behind its winter skin; it is a voyage from the seas of non-being towards the shores of knowledge, and it is a voyage which starts from the Cartesian-like moment of revelation and goes *à la recherche du temps perdu* contained in memory.

Creative imagination always works from memory, yet in various ways and according to the aspect of memory which predominates in a given writer—the two main ones being the visual and the affective. Visual imagination, being more precise than any other form of imagination, is the one which has the greatest admixture of intellect. Everything which pertains to it has been seen through the eyes or conjured up into images from paintings, readings, and from descriptions giving detailed pictures; at the same time the affective impressions attached to those experiences have been formulated in the mind as ideas and concepts, they have become intellectualized, and they are therefore part of the consciousness of the writer. Poetic imagination, visual or affective, can, from images, symbols, visions, and ideas, reach back to the knowledge of the concrete thing, go back to the source of the word which is concrete; it can harmonize the opposing elements of various visions and images into a new yet unseen vision, held together only by the poet's gaze and by his words. But there is a fundamental difference between the two forms of imagination, a difference which is, of course, a matter of degree, for there is no absolutely visual nor absolutely affective imagination, but nevertheless a vital one. The writer who is first and foremost endowed with visual imagination can create new forms, he can transpose details from one tableau to another, he can re-arrange his mnemonic material; but here is the main point: he cannot create at the same time, simultaneously, the feelings experienced as part of the imagined experience, for these feelings have already been intellectualized. The feelings are therefore those remembered, but they are not part and parcel of the whole imaginative experience, which ought to have involved the total consciousness of the poet, who, having ceased to be himself, becomes the words he uses—nothing more but also nothing less. The feelings attached to the experience are there, but like everything else they are summoned ready-made from memory and skilfully clothed in words. The whole thing takes place at a level which excludes that fringe of non-consciousness necessary to poetic creation. Visual imagination enables a writer to start from the present and through a succession of swift, changing tableaux to work towards the past of his childhood, or, starting from an incident in the present, he can link up with the past, and from there work back towards the present. But either in the case of ascending or descending stream, the subject remains separated from those visions and experiences in a present which is isolated from them and a source of suffering and longing for something that has been, will never be again, and will ever remain a memory in a present which is essentially the absence of the past. The creative moment is therefore not a moment of plenitude, but the awareness of the void on the verge of which stands the subject.

Affective memory is like visual memory, never the thing or the experience itself; it is always the identity embodied in words, images, or symbols. The intellect is here, too, involved, consciousness still differentiates between the thing recalled, conjured up, and its original, for if it did not, it would be either hallucination or the dream-state; but here it is not so much a matter of ideas and images, as an upsurge of feelings whence an emotional state as close as possible to the original will arise. The subject is taken out of the present into a world which contains past and future, and which annihilates the present, with of course suffering, but also with the joy that such a transcendental act implies. The subject knows that he exists, and only exists, in the imaginative experience which he lives, but he does not know to start with what he is, or where he is, and he has to work his way out of that state of timelessness towards the present, and a final state of consciousness, which is knowledge—the aim of poetry. The feelings involved here are part of the creative experience, for in affective memory the feelings pertaining to an experience are stored up without being formulated into ideas. The main problem here is for the subject—the poet—to be able to note the swift changes of sensations and the progressive awakening of consciousness in the initial moments when consciousness begins to dawn from the night of non-consciousness, which is the starting point of the poetic experience:

The poet's eye, in a fine frenzy rolling,
Doth glance from heaven to earth, from earth to heaven;
And as imagination bodies forth
The forms of things unknown, the poet's pen
Turns them into shapes, and gives to airy nothing
A local habitation and a name.[1]

The true poet knows only through poetry and does not use poetry to unfold what he already knows. He writes with his whole being, and if one may be forgiven for bringing in the most important source of literary argument in history—*Hamlet*—one might say, as Mr. Eliot said, that Hamlet himself did not know what to do and how to reconcile the apparently irreconcilable conflicts which faced him once his beliefs were destroyed, and once he had realized that what for him could not be, nevertheless was; perhaps the poet himself did not know what to do, to solve on the human plane this apparently insoluble situation.

A poet writes out of himself, with what he has in himself, and, without using the first person, or making of his characters mouthpieces for the expression of his opinions and thoughts, his imagery and metaphors are, and can only be, his own, and they are the very texture of his protean person. We can discover more about the real Shakespeare through a study of his imagery and metaphors than through all the biographies that have been written; the evidence of Dr. C. Spurgeon's work seems to me conclusive on that point; and if we may take one single instance about Racine, *Phèdre* is more illuminating about the feelings of its author than all the historical explanations about his behaviour. Dramatic characters must be deeply rooted in the being of the poet, and they will live only inasmuch as they are imaginative projections of conflicts in their creator's mind. Phèdre shows these signs, and tells us more about Racine than all the records of his household expenses, or his relations' and friends' reminiscences. The essentially religious feeling which underlies the poem is as much Christian as pagan; the sensuousness, the awareness of sin, and the horror of the deed beyond the control of the human being deprived of redeeming grace, are the substance

---

[1] *A Midsummer Night's Dream*, Act V, Scene I.

out of which great saints have been made. The either/or conflict is both Platonic and Christian; whether the spirit wills it or not, the Supreme Will will have his way, and the spirit without grace will be left with the consciousness of the deadly error, and with the knowledge that the triumph of the body in Time could only be temporary, and that it has to return through death to knowledge and Eternity. Phèdre undoubtedly contains aspects, imaginative and real, of her creator. It is the 'objective correlative' which enabled Racine (Christian, believer in God, brought up in the truth, but in rebellion against it owing to the appeal of the senses), to attempt to give expression, through the catharsis of imaginative creation, to his own inner voice. After all, why does a poet accept or 'choose' a given theme? Because there are forces in him which seek expression and weigh upon him, urging him to find the means, symbols, or myths to bring them to life; if not, the poet, haunted by those forces, will have no peace of mind, and will live in 'hell' with the daemons which seek life through him; and in the end the poet cannot but give expression to those forces or be overwhelmed. The true poet is capable of finding the means, myths, or symbols which will enable him to express in a sensuous way, in living characters, the conflicting forces which are in him. The importance of this point is certainly brought out by the readiness of the great poet-dramatists to use any themes or subjects which could be the catalysers of conflicting forces latent in them. . . . As for the Greeks, the themes which they treated were those archetypal knots of human feelings which found an echo in every listener's soul. One may add that the true poet does not write poetry unless he is really *compelled* to do so, because, although the final act of release is pleasant, what precedes—the obsessions, the conflicts, the visions—are awe-inspiring and take him, as a man, to very strange realms. Shakespeare knew something of those feelings, as we may guess from *King Lear*. Rimbaud saw 'Hell' and retraced his steps, and Racine certainly did not stop writing because his worldly ambitions had been satisfied but, more probably, because with Phèdre he had suffered unfathomable agonies, and seen 'the country from whose bourn no traveller returns'. When silence falls upon a poet, it can only be because there are no more voices seeking to break out of himself.

All this is to insist upon the notion that poetry is neither an ornament nor a projection of the superficial creative self into forms, but the essential truth of that self become non-self.

Metre is not by any means poetry, but as it originated with poetry, it remains one of the fundamental attributes of poetry. Any expression of emotion implies a certain rhythm, and when our emotions reach a high pitch of intensity they seem to call forth a certain pattern of rhythm which tends towards regularity of structure. In fact in moments of great emotional stress imaginatively felt by the poet, rhythm can be so important as to be, in extreme cases, sufficient to exteriorize the emotion to the partial neglect of the meaning of the words. In all cases, the structural rhythm of very intense emotions felt by extraordinary men and conveyed in memorable ways forms part of the poetic experience. Rhythm seems to be the most fundamental and primal aspect of human expression, and goes to the source of being. A regular rhythm, a recognizable metre, therefore, gives the listener the essential structure of the emotion or experience which the poet seeks to convey, and helps to create in his mind a state of receptivity whence the poetic experience may arise. That state can be attained only by the sustained use of certain repeated stresses, by a certain music which will detach the listener's mind from its surroundings, from its normal preoccupations, and enable him to live as fully as possible the life of the language he is listening to. It seems to me that in order that such an experience might take place, a partial hypnosis of the mind is necessary; I mean by mind the conscious ego. That partial hypnosis can be obtained by sustained rhythmical pattern or metre, by the use of rhymes, assonances or dissonances at regular intervals, and/or by the high suggestiveness of images and metaphors which transport the listener into worlds beyond his own. The reliance on images and metaphors to the exclusion of other assets of poetry is unsatisfactory on two counts: the first is that no poet can sustain his power of imagery and metaphor for long, and therefore once the flow ceases he falls into flat, unredeemable prose which leaves the reader or the listener completely lost, wondering what will come next; while, on the contrary, if poetry takes place within verse, the rhythm of the verse being constantly maintained, the listener remains in the necessary state of expectancy, and when poetry comes within the verse, the listener is ready to receive it. The second count is that imagination, the power to give life to images and metaphors, is more rare than one thinks, and it is too much to expect to find more than a few people who could reach poetic experience only on those two assets, which are nevertheless the very foundations of poetry.

In poetry meaning is also very important, but the meaning we are seeking in it is different from that of prose. Meaning becomes here a combination of various elements which range from the strictly logical connotations of the words to their auditory, visual associations, along with the music of the line, and of the whole passage which contains the line. One may say that it is no longer strictly speaking a matter of pure meaning, but a matter of meaning within a given climate, colour, or tone. That is true not only of lyrical poetry, where the poet is not primarily concerned with communication, but also of poetic drama, which is written with an audience in mind. The oscillations between meaning and music in Shakespearean acting clearly show the importance of the two elements in poetic drama. Some actors concentrate on the music of the line and use their voices with operatic skill in order to render the Shakespearean music; others concentrate on the meaning or the rhetorical value of the line and, as blank verse can easily break into prose, they sometimes deliver it as prose. The best, like Gielgud in our time, make a successful blend of both elements and maintain meaning within the music of a line which has lost nothing of its original magic.

One might share Claudel's impatience with rhyme which he compares to the ruthless metronome; one can intensely dislike this merciless bell at the end of the line; one can indeed object to feeling like a dog with a tin can tied to its tail; yet one cannot avoid the conclusion which Claudel seems to ignore in his dramatic writings, the fact that poetry implies a definite, recognizable, sustained pattern. Rhythm is one thing, metre is another. The Shakespearean, the Miltonian blank verse, unrhymed, are unfailingly recognizable, so is the Virgilian line, so are the psalms.[1]   Therefore it is difficult to agree with Claudel's wholesale condemnation of French classical prosody. One may find a long poem in alexandrines monotonous, yet it depends upon how the alexandrine is used.   Claudel himself found the first Act of *Britannicus* perfect.   But of course there has been only one Racine.   He alone has succeeded in making the alexandrine walk side by side with prose, or rise to the summits of poetry.   Nobody else has shown the same mastery, the same control over this very difficult line, which, with its wide internal melodic range, has nevertheless a certain stiffness, owing to its syllabic framework and to the rhyme.   The result is that when less masterly hands were laid upon this delicate instrument it broke down; it sagged and dragged with Verlaine, and more often than not it burst into coloured fragments under the strain of Victor Hugo's demands.

French poets and poet-dramatists who came after Racine found themselves in exactly the same plight as English poets who came after Shakespeare and Milton.   After those two masters of the blank verse which, to make things more difficult, Dryden encased in the rhymed couplet, the main preoccupation of poets using that medium was to avoid echoes of Shakespeare and Milton.   This proved in the end an impossible task. Shelley, in *Prometheus Unbound*, produced samples of blank verse which bears the mark of his genius; Keats also, but in *Hyperion* he did not succeed, for long, in avoiding echoes of Milton.   One of the chief reasons why all the attempts at reviving poetic drama at the end of the nineteenth century failed, is that the poet still persisted in trying to use a medium which could no longer be used—blank verse.   Eliot, whose success is the most outstanding in our time, set himself the task of avoiding blank verse and at the same time of evolving a new poetic medium.   Claudel may have entertained similar feelings towards the traditional French verse, he may have felt that with the exception of Rostand in his heroic-comedy, *Cyrano*, nobody in his time had managed to use the alexandrine successfully on the stage; he may have felt, as Supervielle did, that new experiences called for new forms of expression,

[1] De Tonquedec quotes the work of R. F. Condam in *On the Psalms*, p. 202.

and he may have sought to evolve a form which would be entirely his own, a form which has no forerunners in French literature and has only two in the literature of the world—the Bible and Walt Whitman.

Claudel has based his famous theory of free verse or ' verset ', a word which he dislikes, on the rhythm of breathing. The length of a ' verset ', says Claudel, ' corresponds to the time that it takes to breathe in; one breathes out at the end of the line '. In *La Ville* Coeuvre, the poet who speaks for Claudel, says:

> O mon fils! lorsque j'étais un poète entre les hommes,
> J'inventai ce vers qui n'avait ni rime ni mètre,
> Et je le définissais dans le secret de mon coeur cette fonction double
> et réciproque
> Par laquelle l'homme absorbe la vie et restitue, dans l'acte
> suprême de l'expiration,
> Une parole intelligible.

(p. 488, vol. I)

It is strange to note, as De Tonquedec points out in his study on Claudel, that Heredia had said the same thing about the alexandrine. Heredia's words, quoted by A. Poizat, *Le Symbolisme*, I, in *Le Correspondant*, 25th July 1916, are the following: ' It is not as it is believed a line of twelve syllables, it is the ideal line; it spans the normal interval between breathing in and breathing out.' Fervent admirers of Claudel, like Georges Duhamel, defend him on physiological grounds, even though they are compelled to concede the fact that the rhythm of breathing varies according to individuals, and according to the emotion involved. Obviously we are here on extremely slippery ground and heading for a most subjective form of rhetoric. Indeed, one can find in Claudel any number of examples of lines expressing very tempered emotions and yet composed of one single word; one can see that the arrangement on the page has not been imposed by the laws of breathing:

> Si vous songez que vous êtes des hommes et que vous v—
> Ous voyez empêtrés des ces vêtements d'es claves, oh! cri—
> Ez de rage et ne le supportez pas plus longtemps![1]

[1] *Tête d'or*, first version, p. 104.

or

> Ce que je dis, je ne le dis point.   Mais le texte, le texte, le T—
> ——tt texte est là qui le dit.[1]

Mr. Duhamel, trying to defend this kind of writing, says that in the first instance the line is trying to imitate the stutterings of the hero, and in the second it is meant to stress the importance of the text.   One feels nevertheless inclined to say that those are rather puerile devices, unworthy of a serious writer, who happily does not use them often.   The truth is that although Claudel may, like so many poets, try to rationalize his very personal versification, he is a poet who trusts first and foremost in inspiration, without any set rules.   In *Corona* he says that he sings:

> A plein gosier va comme je te pousse,
> Un seul vers si je n'en trouve qu'un dans mon sac, et d'autres
>   qui viennent tous ensemble par secousse.
> Quand il n'y a pas de rime, il faut ma foi, s'en passer.[2]

There is nothing more natural than a poet trusting in inspiration, but just as the gods of old, knowing that they would not be understood, never spoke directly to men, but always spoke through elect individuals such as Tiresias, Cassandra, or some Pythian priestess who could explain their hidden designs to mortals, in the same way the results of inspiration must be embodied in certain forms which are apprehensible to men. Art is imagination and form fused into a kind of oneness, objective enough to be apprehended by other men.   Art is always a compromise between the natural genius of the artist, the time in which he lives, and the medium which he uses; words have a meaning, they have behind them traditions of forms which, although they can be developed, cannot be wiped out by each generation which seeks to make a clean sweep of what preceded it.   Claudel is perhaps too radical in condemning what preceded him; his apologists like Duhamel show perhaps too blind a faith in his innovations.   ' I must confess ', says Duhamel, ' that I cannot always grasp the meaning of Claudel's typography, but knowing the man, I know that he

---

[1] *La Ville*, first version quoted by Duhamel.   [2] *Corona*, p. 186.

only leaves to chance what he likes to leave.' This is perhaps going a bit far, perhaps just as far as De Tonquedec, who, when comparing Claudel with Henri de Régnier, finds Claudel lacking in music. It is obvious that Claudel's verse does not ' sing ' in the way in which Régnier's verse sometimes sings; but then, any sentimental ditty, any arrangement of words based purely on sounds may sing, while some of the most magnificent passages of poetry have their own music, but do not sing. A Beethoven symphony does not sing, some of Shakespeare's short lyrics are the criteria of song, but the splendid music of *Othello, Macbeth,* or *Lear* has nothing to do with the singing quality advocated by De Tonquedec as exemplified by Régnier's poetry.

Claudel's musical phrase is different in structure from the song. His music, based on subtle internal melodies, on the music of images, on the enchantment of sustained metaphors, works on a scale remote from the song. The difficulty, the main difficulty, since we are dealing with drama which is a social art, is that his language, which is most of the time poetic, is not sufficiently dramatic, is not, as it should always be, the instrument of character. The two ideal dramatic languages are that of Racine and that of Shakespeare. The former, spare to the point of being prosaic, direct, transparent, clear, lays bare the human heart in unforgettable accents, or suddenly soars on the wings of rare and so much the more prized metaphors and images; the latter, combining the pithiness of prose with the unique flexibility of the blank verse, closely packs images and metaphors into moments which are within character and also transports characters beyond time. But in his way Shakespeare is as precise and concise as Racine, and when his poetry shoots up in the air, it does so as the rays of a sun, so that it adds to its reality an aura of transcendence. Claudel is too often carried away by elusive images and cosmic metaphors, and the structure of his poetic phrase is, in spite of the domination of ' verset ', something very personal, something in which we often get lost. Blank verse, with its iambic rhythm and its well-marked and easily recognizable stresses, can range easily from the conversational tone to the most inspired moments; the flesh may or may not be there all the time, but the skeleton is always there. The Claudelian ' verset ', if we wish to call it so, is too difficult to recognize. Blank verse and transition from poetry to prose and vice-versa are not as easy in French as they are in English; the rhythm of the French language is more fluid and relies more on the phrase than on the word, and therefore leaves more room than English to rhetoric, and even to arbitrariness of diction. The poetry of Claudel, like much of the poetry of our time, relies perhaps too exclusively on images and metaphors and not enough on structural rhythm. The rhythm of Claudel is above all the rhythm of the images; the result is that very often he achieves beautiful poetry, but which is not on the whole a good medium for drama.

XI

CONCLUDING REMARKS

ONE cannot hope to sum up the whole of Claudel's achievements as a poet dramatist in a few pages. His genius is too
vast and too varied to be enclosed in a few lapidary sentences.
He is one of the heirs of a long tradition which within the French
language stretches from the Greeks to our time and contains
both Racine and Victor Hugo; a tradition which also overflows
national boundaries and embraces the world of Dante and that
of Calderon, that of Shakespeare, and that of Goethe. Yet
although he is part of those vast forces which from the Acropolis
to the Judean Hill have carried mankind forward, his strong
individualism has broken out of old moulds and has laid down
claims which have therefore to be judged mostly on their own
intrinsic merits. With Claudel poetry definitely returns to the
stage, but it is neither the poetry of Racine, the crystal glass
showing us the nakedness and moving pathos of the human
heart, nor the magnificent garb which Victor Hugo's heroes
proudly wear on their shoulders or drag at their heels in tattered
multi-coloured rags. To be sure, the coat which Claudel
wears resembles more than any other has done yet that of
Victor Hugo, but it is nevertheless Claudel's coat, with his
special cut and style of wearing it. True enough, he resembles
Victor Hugo in more than one respect; their imaginations
work on a similar cosmic scale, didactic preoccupations weigh
heavily on their creations and have led them into forcing their
characters through channels which, had they been free from
their author's compulsion, they would not have taken, and also
into speaking with voices which are obviously not their own.
In both cases we have rhetoric, sometimes brilliant, yet often
enough out of character. In both cases we have devices and
contraptions clamped down on themes which cannot bear
them. In both cases we are faced with professions of faith
essentially revolutionary and claiming absolute freedom of

inspiration, yet it must be noted that the importance of the revolution seems to be in reverse ratio to the way the claims are stated.

The violence of language of Victor Hugo's famous prefaces is very mildly echoed by the still traditional enough form and content of his plays. On the one hand, the alexandrine is still there, no longer perhaps the perfect musical phrase, the prodigy of skill, with the fixed beat of a metronome, but rather the exuberant polyphony of a music which overflows the phrase, and sometimes explodes into a shower of notes resembling fireworks. On the other, the search for colourfulness and life-like truth has led him from tragedy to melodrama. Claudel's tone in his didactic writings may be radical, but does not show any trace of rhetorical violence; it clearly and simply conveys the impression that, without any desire to catch the public eye or to pose as the leader of a new literary movement, his sensitiveness cannot find expression through accepted traditional forms and themes. Here we recognize a quality of genuineness and are aware that his quest for new artistic expressions is solely goaded forward by the force of his inner genius, which can come into being only through forms which are essentially his own. One may criticize the esoteric originality of some of Claudel's writings, but one can hardly impugn his sincerity. He is what he is, following the ineluctable force of his inner laws, though one might argue that the same ineluctable internal laws which led Victor Hugo to wear his prophetic and magus' mask has led Claudel to wear the outward signs which mark him as God's man on earth. But then we would become bogged in the unfathomable determinism of human actions and behaviour; so that finally we realize that all we can do is to concern ourselves with the termini, that is to say with actions, behaviour, and their worth. There is no doubt that Claudel has imprinted something original on poetic drama, and one might dare to call it a distinctiveness which it has never had since the days of Racine. There is of course more than one way of being original and of distinguishing oneself from others, but Claudel's way is not that of Alcibiades; it is that of a poet who has a vision of the world which is not, by any means, new—for there is nothing new—but whose external final form bears the mark of the mind and heart which have borne it. But originality—and I mean by originality not the originality of *Ubu Roi*, or even that of *Finnegans Wake*, but the originality which distinguishes the *Phèdre* of Racine from that of Euripides, or *King Lear* from all the various versions which preceded it—is in no way the most important prerequisite of a work of art. There are many other prerequisites, and among them surely one which holds preeminence is the feeling of oneness and harmony embodied in something endowed with life at the level of the essences, and in which all forces and tensions which can tear apart and wreck an ordinary human life have been harmonized into a creation which transcends Time. It seems to me that Claudel's most important works convey that impression of oneness and at a level which has been unsurpassed in France since Racine. Just as in the case of Victor Hugo, we may find it difficult to extricate Claudel's too obvious didactic purpose from the inane rhetoric which surrounds the characters and the poetry of some of his drama; we may also find that while with Victor Hugo we have moved from tragedy to melodrama and to *la pièce à thèse*, with Claudel we have definitely moved from drama and drama-tragedy to miracle- and mystery-plays. Yet in the two greatest plays of Claudel, in the ones where the didactic purpose of the author is reduced to the minimum—*Partage de Midi* and *La jeune fille Violaine* (second version)—pathos and poetry rise to, and maintain, levels unapproached by either of Victor Hugo's best plays—*Ruy Blas* and *Hernani*.

Claudel seems to me to be without doubt the most important French poet-dramatist since Racine. In our time no one in France can challenge his supremacy. During the first half of the twentieth century France has probably produced the most remarkable galaxy of dramatists of any country; indeed, it would be difficult to find anywhere a set of names which could compare with a list which includes Giraudoux, Anouilh, Cocteau, Sartre, Supervielle, Henri Ghéon, etc., yet all those writers, with the exception of Supervielle and Ghéon, have written their plays in prose and can lay no claims to poetic drama; as for those of Supervielle and Ghéon, they are too slender to be placed anywhere near Claudel's. The only country in the Western world in which we find a poet-dramatist whose eminence compares with Claudel's is England: that poet-dramatist is T. S. Eliot. No other dramatic achievements are comparable with theirs, and in the fields of poetic drama the lights which shine from the work of their contemporaries are just as remote from theirs as are those of a fun-fair from the brilliance of stars. In different ways they have laid down claims which no other modern poet-dramatist can offset. If since the great ages of poetic drama—those of Elizabeth and Louis XIV—a few plays have been written which may be regarded as great plays, I should say that these include *The Family Reunion, The Cocktail Party, La jeune fille Violaine, Partage de Midi* and *Le Soulier de Satin.*

Poets cannot be measured with inch-tapes or weighed on heavenly scales. Therefore comparisons between them are impossible, and here I merely wish to suggest what kind of conclusions might be drawn from the examination of some of these two poets' works. Both have dealt with a similar theme, and, above all, both are innovators in dramatic expression.

Claudel and Eliot have dealt with the problem of the saint on the stage, and both have sought to 'justify the ways of God to man', but here the differences are striking, and correspond to the respective attitudes of those two poets to poetry. Where Eliot waits, preparing himself and his reader for the great moments, Claudel shoots up from nowhere into the sky or pounces on his quarry, tears it to pieces, and disappears again we know not where. While both know 'that Destiny waits in the hand of God', Claudel, swept away by an apocalyptic force which carries him to the 'burning bush', becomes that very hand which chastises and torments and rewards his fellow beings whose lives are mere mathematical signs of the vast Claudelian synthesis, while Eliot remembers the reverence and the mystery and approaches his Maker with the humility of one who knows and does not know, and yet who hopes that the ineffable moment may come, as come it does. Both Rodrigue and Becket are proud men who have to be brought within God's Will. But what a difference! We have only to think of the complexity, anthropomorphism, and didacticism of the first to realize the simplicity, the sinlessness, the

[169]

supreme detachment of the second. In *Le Soulier de Satin*
God has to use all his power and resourcefulness to bring these
elect of His back to Him and to His chosen Church on earth;
in the second—*Murder in the Cathedral*—God does not need to
bait, beguile, torment, and coerce His creatures into Heaven;
Becket, like Christ, has come to earth with his appointed task:
he knows that the human will must be surrendered to the
Eternal pattern—to God's Will—and he knows that he must
testify, by his sacrifice, to God's interest in, and love for men,
and that it is by his sacrifice that God's purpose will be achieved,
as it was achieved in Christ. Eliot has wisely realized that one
cannot dramatize sainthood, that the saint who comes closer and
closer to ' the still point of the turning world ' cannot be tossed
about by human passions, and that actions and events can only
be like pale reflections of the more profound and truly eternal
life. The closer we come to Divinity the more action and word
tend towards oneness; in the saint their respective positions
are reversed from those they hold in the average man, for
action can only be in the saint the last flicker of a very nearly
still life. *Murder in the Cathedral* partakes of the morality play
and also of Greek tragedy, and the Greeks knew the eternity
of certain emotions which poetry alone could convey, they also
knew that action was a mere ripple of that deep sea. *Le Soulier
de Satin* is perhaps in the last resort an epic *ad majorem religionis
Romanae gloriam*, a rather incomplete transfiguration of man's
suffering.

The problem of dramatic expression is in this case the most
important of all, for it determines the vital point of the relationship between author and audience, a relationship which is the
foundation of dramatic art. Eliot may not have the cosmic
vision of Claudel, he may not have the rise, the roll, the carol,
the creation of Hopkins, or the purely verbal music of Swinburne, but he has a full measure of all those gifts, and he has,
besides this, that mysterious innate knowledge of the human
heart which was part of the greatness of Racine and of Baudelaire. He has also the seeing eye and the secret which Wordsworth alone seems to have known, of those meditative melodies
whose music can lift the soul into the pattern and movement of
unchanging things. He has succeeded in solving the two great

problems which have partially eluded Claudel's grasp—the problem of versification for the stage, and the problem of reviving tragedy. The extreme flexibility of his verse ranges from the taut, pithy language of the first scene of *The Cocktail Party* to the pervading poetry of its second Act, and to the moving and beautiful poetry of the choruses of *Murder in the Cathedral*. That poetry gives one the feeling of watching the progress of a thoroughbred horse which, whether walking or trotting, displays the perfect working of a well-controlled and powerful instrument and one which might in a moment of ardour gallop out of sight. Claudel's poetic diction offers no middle course; his poetry lives only when it is in full flight. Then it can soar very high, perhaps higher than other verse of our time, but when the flight ceases we fall to the ground, half-dead, and then we spend long moments of boredom and drudgery preparing for the next flight. His poetry has no vertebrae to hold it erect, waiting for life to flow in it; either the spirit is there and raises it, or it is nothing. With him we never have the complex experience of watching a perfect instrument which, even in repose, can give us a hint of its tremendous possibilities; there is no repose, no slow motion, only fantastic gales which might blow one off the earth. As he does not work within recognizable patterns, and as he relies entirely on the musical and visual rhythms of the emotions, it is only when the spirit blows that we have poetry, but then it is poetry of a very high order, and one which in some of his best plays can span distances. But in an age when prose is the norm of literary expression, poetic drama has to compete with prose drama, and it can do so only on the latter's ground, in plays which show that poetry is not only part of character but can rise beyond character towards a form of beauty and a wealth of experience which prose cannot reach. This never arises where poetry is used for poetry's sake, for this is something which in the plain man's mind implies its condemnation because it is too remote from everyday life and is artificial. Claudel has evolved a form of poetic drama such that he himself has only very seldom been capable of transcending its limitations, and then thanks to his extraordinary gift as a poet. After him one can put up a notice: ' No through road '. Eliot, on the contrary, has kept the road open; he has consciously trimmed poetic language to the criteria of dramatic expression and characters, and has endeavoured to blend the suggestive range of poetry with the directness and easy apprehensibility of prose language, so that he is not only the builder of great harmonious constructions, but the founder of new ones. He is, like Claudel, great by his achievement; yet he is more, for he can only gain by the light which will shine forth from his progeny. Both have gone further than any other poet-dramatists since Shakespeare and Racine towards restoring poetry to its former pre-eminence on the stage. Eliot has sought to and succeeded in reconciling dramatic communication and music of language. He has gone as far as possible towards eliciting perceptions of a reality which belongs to the world of imagination without losing contact with the everyday world. Claudel, carried away on the wings of his poetic genius, has conveyed his dramatic and tragic effects not so much through a language which rises naturally from the object which inspires it, as through the stirring force of the images and metaphors which fill the poet's mind. He has given us splendid visions of a reality beyond the senses, but he is on the whole so remote from the everyday world, that a poet who wished to use him as a springboard would have to retrace his steps from the beatific vision of Beatrice, towards the plain world of the *selva oscura* where Dante met Virgil.

NOTE I

THE rise of rationalism from the Renaissance onwards has slowly led to man's isolation from transcendence, and to his tragedy. In the seventeenth century, the age which begins with Descartes and Milton, transcendence remains, but on the whole Creator and creation are separated, reason has driven between them a gap which only intuitive experience continuously renewed can bridge. From then on man ceases to be one, the division between the affective and the rational has begun, yet although the temporal is always on the verge of disappearing into nothingness, it is still connected with the Eternal in moments of grace or of intuitive apprehension of existence. In the eighteenth century the separation between Creator and creation reaches its climax. In the immanent universe in which he lives, man asserts his existence by the powers of his heart and by his reason, which can control history and master his surroundings. From the eighteenth century onward man is on the whole separated from transcendence, but he has faith in the light of reason and he is optimistic; he is not dismayed; he feels that reason can apprehend the ambient reality and that language can express it. There is no feeling of tragedy, the loss of transcendence is not yet felt, and immanence suffices. The historical disorders and the upheavals of the end of that century and of the beginning of the nineteenth showed that reason could no longer control human destiny and that history transcended reason, that it had a transcendence of its own (cf. Hegel). Then man began to feel his loneliness, his solitude; he realized the failure of rationalism and objectivism, and he sought to understand the universe through himself; yet with the awareness that he could never be what he wanted to be, that his past and his future, of which he constantly caught glimpses, constantly eluded him, and that therefore he was ever condemned to live on the verge of a vacuum which nothing could fill, nothing except perhaps death. Nevertheless, he still felt that he could apprehend through himself the mystery of the universe, and that he could express it through art. Although conscious of his isolation, God-like in some ways or daemonic, he had not lost faith in his powers, which tended to be more and more intuitive rather than rational.

The development of science which took place during the second half of the nineteenth century soon restored the balance in favour of reason, but not for long; this time it was the last glow before the collapse, the St. Martin's Summer of reason—science only proved to man his boundless ignorance and his insignificance. We were soon back to the anxiety of Pascal without the refuge of faith—a vast, terrifying universe, awe-inspiring, pregnant with all kinds of means to destroy man and his ways, and nothing, nobody to turn to for salvation. Thence the sense of fear and tragedy, the end of certitudes, the beginning of anxious questionings, the beginning of our age of 'Angst'. In that state of isolation and fear man could no longer ignore the sense of transcendence, yet he knew that it was completely beyond him and that nothing could connect his temporal tragedy with the Eternal, for the Incarnation had long been forgotten. Thence his awareness that he could no longer master the universe and express it through art, his realization that he could only hint at the mystery and hint at it subjectively, with the feeling

[173]

that the microcosm which he was might surely reflect something of the awe-inspiring macrocosm, but he knew more and more that there was no meeting-point of Time and Eternity except in art, which became transcendent, annihilating the contingent in order to assert the existence of Being (Mallarmé, Valéry). Thence also, later on, his flight from fear into the irrational world of surrealism.

Now that all aspects of scientific thought (physical science, nuclear physics, cosmology) and philosophy tend to assert the oneness of life and the interdependence of man and the universe, man realizes more and more that transcendence must again be closely and continuously linked with Time. Without it man is only a husk, Time only a shade, and history the record of shadowy gestures taking place in Eternity. Man alone, the meeting-point of Time and Eternity, can give these shadows their substance and restore to history its pentecostal force. For that, man must remember what has been; he must remember that the rock which, Sisyphus-like, he restlessly rolls is that same rock which was pushed away from Christ's sepulchre; he must remember that, if the moon and Mars and other planets are still undescried by human eyes, all the landscapes of the mind are part of the memories of God which slowly come to light through history. He must remember that life is neither the Danaids' barrel which can never be filled up, nor the blind goddess who rolls man forward along his ineluctable path, but that it is a living substance of which man is the consciousness, and as such he has the means, through his will and his faith, to hear the distant voices, to see the dim lights, and in moments of intensity to rise towards the essences to which he belongs and towards which he moves; in these moments, which are the yeast of human life, fear has no place, for they are the moments when transcendence comes into Time.

NOTE II

Dramatic and lyrical poetry

The greatest poetry of mankind is dramatic poetry; that includes the poetry of Homer, Dante, and Milton, as well as that of Shakespeare and Racine, who are sometimes described in an incomplete way as dramatists. Even the most purely lyrical poetry, such as the poetry of Donne, Burns, Villon or Verlaine, is dramatic, for nobody could deny such a quality to the anguished sonnets of Donne or to the passionate love-poetry of Burns or of Baudelaire. Homer's poetry was, as we all know, the narration of great deeds in themselves dramatic. It was like the poetry of the ballads and the lyrical songs of the Middle Ages, a poetry of action, a poetry rising directly from the intensity of language, conveying accounts of heart-rending events and profoundly moving feelings. In the *Divina Commedia* it is only in Heaven, where everything is fixed, unchangeable, intent, that there is no drama, no conflicting tensions; and Heaven is the human aim of poetry. With the exception of the very last cantos of *Il Paradiso*, which form the apex of the work, and embody the sublime, indescribable experience of a being who has lived the eternal moment and has been dazzled by the whiter than the white, the greater part of the work is composed of dramatic moments, which have been fully exploited by composers and dramatists. Dante's poetry is essentially dramatic. He uses symbols, allegories, and visions which, in his time, were often acted or mimed inside or in front of churches; but he is, above all, the greatest visionary poet of all times, and his visions are so intense that language—direct language—burned and became the vision and the music of his great poem. It is the poet who forms the foundation and the corner-stone of the edifice, and the poetry, lyrical and therefore dramatic —for lyricism is dramatic conflict—rises from the poet's self torn by conflicting forces, while he is also in conflict with the opposing forces of other selves, and only reaches plenitude, the pure flight and full reconciliation of the end, when he can say: *in la sua voluntade e nostra pace*, when his self has merged into the white shaft of the burning sun. His words are in themselves images without any need of similes, the metaphors add richness and complexity to the depth of vision, and the whole poem is based on a symbol containing other symbols which are knots or archetypes of human sensitiveness and which give that complex creation its extraordinary poetic power.

There is no need to stress the dramatic quality of Milton's great poems. *Samson Agonistes*, with its choruses and actors, was meant to be, and is a drama. As for *Paradise Lost*, it is well known that Milton hesitated for a long time between the epic and the directly dramatic form, and that it was only in the end that he came to the wise conclusion that the age of the ' mysteries ' was passed, and that such a subject could never be treated adequately upon a real stage.

If the names of Wordsworth, Lucretius, and Goethe have not been mentioned, it is not because they are not among the great, but simply because they are poet-philosophers, and because they have not completely succeeded in detaching their work from themselves. There are, of course, strong doctrinal and philosophical views in the poetry of Dante and Milton, but their primary concern was not to expound their philosophy. In both cases the philosophy, the thought, is the framework of the poetry, which rises beyond it in that breadth of emotions, that depth of experience and universality which are valid for all men, and for all time. Of course, one is bound to say that Shakespeare alone, amongst the greatest, has truly been the poet 'protean' whose poetry has risen from the things themselves, from the symbols, actions, feelings, and emotions which he sought to express, while he was the medium of expression, the catalyser who made the poetry possible. He had, in a supreme degree, the great gift of the poet—the imagination which enabled him to be everything; he could return to the sources of Life, and his heart could throb with the life of a tree, of a villain, or of a noble mind, and he could, when he wanted, be the lover watching stars falling through his fingers with the same innocence and freshness of feelings as a plain man watching crumbs of bread falling to the ground towards hungry birds. That does not mean that the man Shakespeare was an abstraction, a non-being who existed only in his poetry. Far from it. The man and the poet are always one in the act of poetry. But just as children, self-contained in a life of their own, may be completely different from their parents, and yet have something—indefinable perhaps, but none the less real—which relates them to the same source, similarly the creations of a poet, though they may be masterpieces endowed with a life of their own, have something which links them with their creator—and that something is the words. The poet makes with words, and the way he arranges them, the way he uses them, bears traces of the heart and mind where those words have lived or through which they have passed, for in the end they are that very heart and mind. The spirit may blow from afar, from the very Sources, but the voice which it has chosen is a human voice, which has unmistakably recognizable tones.

True poetry does not leave much room for the conscious expression of a philosophy; it has a wholeness which excludes the limitations of any system; it is life *essentialized* and *universalized*, and the poet is the medium which expresses it.

Had it not been for the existence of Dante one might have been able to say that the greatest dramatists were also the greatest poets; and there would have been plenty of evidence to support such a view—Aeschylus, Sophocles, Shakespeare, Racine. They wrote at different times and therefore their artistic conventions were different; but their poetry rises from identical sources which are the great conflict between the eternal and the temporal, and the pathos born from the realization that the supreme consciousness, the revelation of eternity, however moving and painful, is in the temporal, whose greatest glory is to be the instrument of Destiny and to know it. This implies a metaphysical view of the universe, and applies to Prometheus and Antigone as well as to Anthony or Phèdre. The authors of these creations could not have felt and depicted the drama, the ' duality ' of the human situation, unless they were poets. Being poets, great poets, they could not but have a sense of drama; they could not but see the sharp edges, the violent contrast of things; they could not fail to be dramatic. Although Wordsworth and Coleridge did not write for the stage, there is drama in *The Rime of the Ancient Mariner* or in *The Ode on Intimations of Immortality.*

Drama is in the self, dramatic poetry is lyrical and cannot but be lyrical, and it seems to me true to say that no dramatic character is truly alive and great who is not the result of some profoundly conflicting feelings and thoughts which have lived, or still live, in the consciousness and sub-consciousness of his creator. There lies the difference between the genuine experience and the second-hand experience which may produce poetry of a certain level, but which lacks what Hopkins described so aptly as the rise, the roll, the creation. If I were asked to try to say precisely what I meant by lyrical poetry, I would say that lyrical poetry seems to me to be by definition the imaginative solution of conflicts and contrasts. It rises from a division, and ever expresses the drama of the soul divided against itself, from others, or from an earthly or heavenly Eden which it seeks to reach. The lyrical moment is the creation, imaginative, and therefore more real than the real, of what has not been and will never be; it takes place at a point where the tension rises from the harrowing conflicts which rage in the suffering self in the present which has become universal, and in that moment of supreme vision it knows that its fulfilment, which might have been or could be, can exist only in the mind and will have no to-morrow; and all the might-have-been's or could-be's add to and renew the creative tension. The lyrical moment is the point of supreme consciousness annihilating all in a timeless moment, the ashes of which are poetry.

Jung said something similar when he wrote: ' All creativeness in the realm of the spirit . . . arises from a state of mental suffering, and it is spiritual stagnation, psychic sterility which causes this state.' Yeats believed that poetry, ' that terrible beauty ', was born from suffering. T. S. Eliot, in his essay on Dante, says that amongst the other difficulties which stood in the way of his enjoyment of *Il Paradiso*, there was ' the pre-judice that poetry not only must be found through suffering, but can find its materials only in suffering '. He said that about *Il Paradiso*, which is a poem of joy, a sensuous apprehension of divine blessedness. I wonder if Eliot's fundamental objection can be disposed of by the example of *Il Paradiso*, for not only do I feel that the poet as a being in Time cannot but live through a certain amount of suffering and ' Angst ' at the sight of the divinity and the state of blessedness which he witnesses and which one day might or might not be his, but above all, as Eliot himself says, there is the point that ' the states of improvement and beatitude which Dante describes are still further from what the modern world can conceive as cheerfulness, than are his states of damnation '. We are not dealing here with human cheer-fulness or joy, but with the supra-human feeling of elation experienced by a great soul inward bent, and realizing in timeless moments the awe-inspiring journey which Life, born from Eternity, has blissfully gone through before it can be dissolved once more into the divine flame of all knowing and fixed joy. On the plane of Life, whether the source of joy is human or divine, as in the mystical experience, the emotion is all, and it implies a complete obliteration of self and will into the timeless moment when nothing but that emotion exists; it is a moment which can only be described as a mnemonic recollection, a very incomplete reflection of the original experience: *O quanto è corto il dire, e come fioco al mio concetto.* Those are the words which precede the description of a mystical experience in one of the highest peaks which poetry has ever reached. Only Dante has succeeded in conveying the experience of a light brighter than any human eye can sustain. On the contrary, mental suffering arises from conflicts and contrasts of emotions, or individual will set against Supreme Will, together with the intense aware-ness of the self in moments when he views simultaneously his whole past and future, and realizes that it neither is nor will ever be what he wants it to be, and that he must either suffer eternally that wound, or seek reconciliation and joy—passive and active—by surrendering to the Supreme Will. Art is one of the means by which one can bring about a reconciliation—a solution of those conflicts into oneness—and merge the self, source of consciousness and suffering, into the transcendentalism of creation which is joy, but a joy which never survives the moment of creation, a joy which dies in the moment of awakening, when one returns to the world of human time. As in joy, the conflicting elements of the emotions have been incorporated into something beyond the personal, something which has been essentialized and univer-salized, which is an organic whole, and which is the work of art.

Art is unreal—that is to say it offers us the reality of the artist, which is more complete than the reality apprehended by the senses and assessed by science can ever be, for it contains both. Art being unreal, the work of art is necessarily composed of symbols which will summon images of sensuous reality or imaginative visions and harmonies which will have a more real, a more essential reality than that of the senses or of any scientific data. Any significant work of art, whatever its theme—joyful or sad—produces an æsthetic emotion which is always tinged with sadness and can easily resolve itself into complete sadness, as is the way with any intense emotion caused by artistic creation. That seems to be due to the realization that here we have something truly beautiful, but which exists only in the intense moments of intuitive creation. A work of art is indeed born in moments of intensity, in the course of which the creative mind has a depth of vision whose scope might embrace the whole picture of man's relation with the universe, and his unavoidable fate. The more powerful the creative imagination, the greater the synthesis and the wider and deeper its power of suggestion, and one cannot but be profoundly moved to the point of sadness by such an insight in life and in its finitude. Art is what is not, a synthesis of essentials, a pro-jection of the true being, but a projection which can only be fleetingly apprehended in rare moments and which cannot fail to permeate the sub-conscious with a feeling of sadness. It exists only through the medium of life, and is part of life; it is that part of life which gives birth to what is time-less, and thus transcends life and links it with its Source. Beauty in art is always moving to the point of sadness; I mean by beauty a creation which not only satisfies man's æsthetic sense of harmony for lines, sounds, and colours, but a creation which gives birth in the observer, the listener, or reader, to an experience which goes to the very source of the person at the meeting point of being and pure Being. A true work of art is an entity, an object which imposes itself as a whole on our subjectivity, marking it, modifying it; this is therefore an operation which involves a temporary subjugation of the individual self merging into the Great One, and cannot take place without that conscious or subconscious suffering which is born from the dim awareness that this vision of Eternity is only a brief moment which will not last, and might never recur.

BIBLIOGRAPHY

(Most of these works are published by: Gallimard, édition de la N.R.F.)

1882–1883   *L'Endormie.*
1887   *Le Sombre Mai, Chanson d'Automne* (*Corona benignitatis anni Dei*).
1888   *Une Mort Prématurée.*
1889   First version of *Tête d'Or.*
1890   First version of *La Ville.*
1892   *La jeune fille Violaine.*
1893–1894   *L'Échange.*
1894–1895   Second version of *Tête d'Or.*
1895–1900   *Poèmes en prose.* (First part of *Connaissance de l'Est*, REVUE DE PARIS, REVUE BLANCHE, L'OCCIDENT, LE MERCURE DE FRANCE.)
1895   *Vers d'Exil.*
1896   *L'Agamemnon d'Eschyle* (translation). *Le Repos du Septième Jour.*
1897   Second version of *La Ville.*
1898   Second version of *La jeune fille Violaine.*
1900   First part of *Les Muses.*
        Développement de l'Eglise.
1901–1905   *Connaissance de l'Est* (Second part).
1901   Publication of *L'Arbre* which contains the early plays except for the first versions of *Tête d'Or*, of *La Ville*, and of *La jeune fille Violaine.*
1903   *Connaissance du Temps.*
1904   *Traité de la Connaissance au Monde et de Soi-Même.*
1905   *Ténèbres. Obsession.*
        Partage de Midi.
        Ballade (*Corona benignitatis*).
        L'Esprit et l'Eau.
        Positions et Propositions, II.
1907   *Magnificat.*
        La Muse qui est la grâce.
        Processionnal pour saluer le Siècle nouveau.
1908   *La Maison Fermée.*
1909   *L'Otage. Ma conversion. St-Jacques le Majeur.*
        Charles-Louis Philippe (*Corona benignitatis*).
        Sous le Signe du Dragon.
1910   *Lettre au Père Ubald* (*Positions et Propositions, II*).
        Propositions sur la Justice.
        La Physique de l'Eucharistie.
        Ière note sur les Anges.
        L'Annonce faite à Marie.
1911   *Lettre à Sylvain Pitt sur St-Joseph* (*Positions et Propositions, II*).
        La Cantate à trois voix.
1913   First version of *Protée. Strasbourg. Sainte Odile. Chant de la St-Louis* (*Corona benignitatis anni Dei*).
1914   *L'Offrande du temps.*
        Le Pain dur.
1915   *La Nuit de Noël 1914.*

1915   *Aux Morts des Armées de la République.*
      Tant que vous voudrez, mon général.
      La Grande Attente.
      Si Pourtant.
      Sainte Thérèse.
1916   *Le Père humilié.*
1917   *Ballade (feuilles de Saints).*
      L'Ours et La Lune.
      L'homme et son désir.
      La Messe là-bas.
1918   *L'architecte. Sainte Geneviève. St-Louis.*
1919   *Dessins.* Introduction to several works (Lecture given at the théâtre du Gymnase). *Lettre à Alexandre Cingria sur la Décadence de l'Art sacré.*
1919–1924   *Le Soulier de Satin.*
1920   *Sur la Mode.*
      Saint-Georges (feuilles de Saints).
1921   *Ode Jubilaire pour le 600ème anniversaire de la mort de Dante.*
      A la memoire de l'Abbé Daniel Fontaine.
      Adieu au Danemark.
      Du mal et de la liberté.
1922   *Poèmes au verso de Sainte Geneviève.*
1923   *La Femme et son ombre* (second version).
      A travers les villes en flammes.
1925   *Réflexions et propositions sur le vers Français. La Philosophie du Livre.*
1926   Second version of *Protée.*
      Hang Tchéou.
      Le poète et le Shamisen.
      Lettre au Professeur Miyajima.
      La Maison du Pont-des-Faisans.
      Jules, ou l'homme aux deux cravates.
      L'Abîme Solaire.
      Les heures du Foyer.
      Richard Wagner.
      Sainte Jeanne d'Arc.
      Correspondance avec Jacques Rivière, 1907–1914.
1927   *Et toi, que penses-tu du Christ?*
      Sous le rempart d'Athènes.
      Du côté de la défense.
      Le livre de Christophe Colomb.
      Religion et Poésie.
      Lettre à l'Abbé Brémond sur l'inspiration poétique.
1927–1933   *L'Apocalypse* (first exegesis).
      Figures et Paraboles.
      Les aventures de Sophie.
1928   *Les invités a l'attention.*
      Le voleur volé.
1929   Speech to the Catholic actors of New York.
      Préface aux ' Oeuvres ' d'Arthur Rimbaud.
1931   *La Confession.*
      Saint Tarcision.
      Le départ de Lao-Tseu.
1932   *Note sur l'art Chrétien.*
      L'Eglise, maison de prière.
      Autre fragment sur Saint-Joseph.
      Smara.

BIBLIOGRAPHY

1932 *La Pérégrination Nocturne.*
      Seconde note sur les Anges.
1933 *Sensation du Divin.*
      Hommage à Liége.
      Hommage à Anvers.
      Two lectures to Belgian men of letters.
      La Parabole du Festin (First version).
      Un poète regarde la Croix.
1934 *Pâques.*
      La Nuit de Pâques.
      Les instruments mystiques.
      La voix humaine.
1935 *Introduction à la peinture hollandaise.*
      Ste Thérèse de Lisieux.
      Le Saint-Esprit.
      Au Confluent de la Musique.
      Un regard en arrière.
      Conversations dans le Loir et Cher.
1933–35 *Jeanne au Bûcher* (music by Honegger).
      Le Festin de la Sagesse (second version of *La Parabole du Festin*).
1936 *Le nom.*
      La Papouasie.
      Vendredi Saint.
      Le Monastère.
      La Motocyclette.
      Consolation à une mère sur la mort de sa fille.
      L'Avion et la diplomatie.
      L'Epée et le miroir.
1937 *Vitraux des Cathédrales de France.*
      Jean Steen.
      La Chanson française.
      Du sens figuré de l'Ecriture.
      Mon Pays.
      Le goût du fade.
      L'Anarchie dirigée.
      Le Plaidoyer pour le Corps.
      Louis Veuillot.
      L'Etoile collective.
      Sainte Lucie.
1938 *La Circoncision.*
      Saint Jean Bosco.
      Aux Lépreux de l'Hôpital Saint Louis.
      Aux Jeunes Gens de 1938.
      Une visite à Bâle.
      L'Enfant Jésus de Prague.
      Le Poison Wagnérien.
      La Mort de Francis Jammes.
      Les Contemplatrices de l'Orient.
      Le Chant Religieux.
      Le Bienfait de la contradiction.
      Le visage du Christ.
      Le Régime du Bonheur.
1939 *Introduction au livre de Ruth.*
      Le Pape Pie XI.
      Le Couronnement de Pie XII.

[181]

1939 *Charles Péguy.*
La Cathédrale de Strasbourg.
Un après-midi à Cambridge.
Moab ou le recul d'Israël.
La Prophétie des Oiseaux.
Sainte Catherine.
Watteau.
L'Indifférent.
1941 *Jordaens.*
Les quatre Evangélistes.
La lecture.
1942 *Seigneur, apprenez-nous à prier.*
La vocation de Saint Louis.
Sur la Musique.
Présence et prophétie.
1943 *Les Psaumes et la Photographie.*
1944 *La vision de la Chandeleur.*
Sur le Père Antoine Marc Falaize.
Arthur Honegger.
1946 *La Rose et le Rosaire.*
La Vierge de Moissac.
Introduction à l'Apocalypse (Egloff).
Le livre de Job (Plon).
1935–1953 *Claudel contemple l'Apocalypse.*
Paul Claudel interroge le Cantique des Cantiques (not yet published, 1954).
Dodoitzu.
La légende de Prâkriti.
Cent phrases pour éventails.
Saint François.
Bestiaire Spirituel.
Discours et Remerciements.
Contacts et Circonstances.
1949 *Correspondance avec André Gide, 1899–1926.*
Accompagnements.
1954 *Mémoires improvisés.*

SELECTED LIST OF WORKS, ARTICLES
AND ESSAYS

Ancelet-Hustache, Jeanne, *Pos. et Prop.*, II. *Nouvelles littéraires*, Sept. 29, 1934.

Angers, Pierre, ' Commentaire à l'art poétique de Paul Claudel '. Paris, *Mercure de France*, 1949.

Barjon, Louis, *L'Oeuvre de Paul Claudel*, saisie totale de l'univers. *Cité Nouvelle*, Lyon, March 15–May 10, 1941.

Beaumont, Ernest, ' Claudel and the problem of love '. *Dublin Review*, First Quarter, 1951.

Benda, Julien, *La France Byzantine*. N.R.F., pp. 262–267.

Bidou, Henri, *Revue de Paris*, April 15, 1936.

Bindel, Victor, *Claudel et nous*. Casterman, 1947.

Bounoure, G., ' *Le Soulier de Satin* ' par Paul Claudel. N.R.F., Vol. I, pp. 129–141.

— *L'oiseau dans ' Le Soleil Levant'* par Paul Claudel. N.R.F., Vol. 2, pp. 630–640.

Brasillach, Robert, *Revue Universelle*, Nov. 15, 1935.

Bruckberger, R. E., *Ligne de faîte*. Paris, Gallimard, 1942, 143 pp.

Calvet, J., *Le renouveau catholique dans la littérature contemporaine*. Lanore.

Carrouges, Michel, *Eluard et Claudel*. Paris, édit. du Seuil, 1945, in-16, 151 pp.

Chaigne, Louis, *Vies et oeuvres d'écrivains*. Vol. I, Lanore.

— *La Rencontre de Paul Claudel*. Paris, Lethielleux, 1942, 32 pp. *Publicistes chrétiens*, No. 6.

Charpentier, John, *L'Evolution de la poésie lyrique de Joseph Delorme à Paul Claudel*. O.R., Paris, 1930.

Claudel, Paul, ' Jeanne d'Arc au Bûcher, conférence '. *Conferencia*, Oct. 1, 1936, pp. 397–407.

Clouard, Henri, *La Poésie française moderne*. Gauthier-Villars.

Copeau, Jacques, *Souvenirs de Théâtre*.

— *Les femmes dans le théâtre de Claudel*. *Conferencia*, Vol. I, pp. 519–538.

Crémieux, Benjamin, ' *L'Otage* '. *Je suis partout*, Nov. 3, 1934.

Desroches, Le P. H.-Ch., *Paul Claudel, poète de l'amour*. Paris, édit. du Cerf, 1944, 168 pp. *Le Coeur et la Croix*, 2.

De Tonquedec, Joseph, *L'Oeuvre de Paul Claudel*. Beluchesne.

Du Bos, Charles, *Approximations*, Sixième série. Paris, Correa, 1934.

Duhamel, Georges, *Paul Claudel*. Mercure de France.

Dumont, G. and Amoudru, B., *Paul Claudel missionnaire*. Lille, édit. Sam, 1944.

Ferrare, Henri, *La trajectoire claudélienne*. Paris, Cahiers des poètes catholiques, 1940.

Friche, Ernest, *Etudes claudéliennes*, Vol. I. Porrentruy, 1943.

Ganne, Pierre, ' Bergson et Claudel ', in *Henri Bergson*, essais et témoignages inedits. 2nd ed., Neuchâtel, 1941, pp. 294–310.

Ghéon, Henri, ' Quinze ans de théâtre sur le plan chrétien '. *Revue des Jeunes*, May 15, 1936.

Gide, André, *L'Evolution du théâtre*, with Introduction by Carl Wildeman. Manchester Univ. Press.

Gillet, Louis, *Pos. et Prop.*, II. *L'Echo de Paris*, May 30, 1935.

— *Claudel présent*. Fribourg, 1942, 105 pp.

— *Claudel, Péguy*. Paris, Editions du Sagittaire, 1946.

Gouhier, Henri, ' *L'Otage* à la Comédie Française '. *Revue des Jeunes*, Nov. 15, 1934.

Grandeur de Paul Claudel, by F. Jammes, C. F. Ramuz, J. Schlumberger, Louis Massignon, Ch. A. Weidle, Ch. du Bos, D. de Rougemont. N.R.F., Vol. 2, Dec. 1936.

Huby, Joseph, *Claudel devant l'univers*. *Les Cahiers de Neuilly*, Book IX, pp. 10–24.

Jouve, Raymond, *Comment lire Paul Claudel*. Paris, édit. ' Aux étudiants de France', 1946.

Lalou, René, *Paul Claudel*. *Revue de Paris*, Vol. 4, pp. 357–382.

Lanson, Gustave, *Corneille*.

— *La tragédie classique*.

Larbaud, Valéry, *Sous l'invocation de Saint Jérome*. N.R.F., pp. 130–132, 245.

Lasserre, Pierre, *Les Chapelles littéraires*. Garnier.

Lavaud, B., ' Un poète habite la Bible'. *Revue Thomiste*, Oct. 1938.

Lefèvre, Frédéric, *Les Sources de Paul Claudel*. Lemercier, Paris, 1927.

Lemaitre, Jules, *Jean Racine*.

Madaule, Jacques, *Le Génie de Paul Claudel—Le Drame de Paul Claudel*. Desclée-De Brouwer.

— *Reconnaissances*. Paris, Desclée-De Brouwer, 1943. Cf. *Claudel, poète solaire. Rencontres*, 1941.

Martin du Gard, Maurice, ' *L'Otage*'. *Nouvelles Littéraires*, Nov. 10, 1934.

Massin, Jean, *Les échos de Saint-Maurice*, Oct. 1935; *Le Courrier de Genève*, Nov. 9, 1935; *Le livre de Christophe Colomb, Hommage à Paul Claudel, La vie intellectuelle*, July 10, 1935.

Mauriac, François, *Réponse au discours de réception*. March 13, 1947.

Maurois, André, *Etudes littéraires françaises*, 2 vols. Paris, Sfelt, 1947.

Méchin, Benoist and Blaizot, Georges, *Bibliographie des oeuvres de Paul Claudel* (1890–1929). Paris, A. Blaizot, 1931.

Meunessier, R. P., ' Contemplation claudélienne '. *Revue des Jeunes*, May 15, 1935.

Molitor, André, *Aspects de Paul Claudel*. Paris, Desclée-De Brouwer, 1945.

Nichol, Allardyce, *The World Drama*.

O'Flaherty, Kathleen, *Paul Claudel and ' The Tidings brought to Mary '*. Cork Univ. Press, 1948.

Onillon, Abbé Jacques, *Par ' l'Annonce faite à Marie ' de Paul Claudel*. Angers, Siraudeau, 1944, 103 pp.

Peacock, Ronald, *The Poet in the Theatre*. Routledge.

Perche, Louis, *Claudel et les grandes odes*. Périgueux, 1945.

Perrin, E. Sainte-Marie, *Introduction à l'oeuvre de Paul Claudel*. Paris, Bloud et Gay, 1926.

Pesquidoux, Joseph de, *Sol de France*. Paris, Plon, 1942.

Peyre, Henri, *Le classicisme de Paul Claudel*. N.R.F., Sept., 1932.

Prévost, Jean, *Les Eléments du drame de Paul Claudel*. N.R.F., May, 1929.

Raymond, Mercel, *De Baudelaire au Surréalisme*. Paris, Corti, 1947.

Resel, Paul, *Paul Claudel, dramaturge chrétien*. Paris, Edit. du Temps Présent, 1941, 64 pp.

Rodot, Robert Valéry, *Préface à une anthologie de la poésie catholique*. Paris, 1916.

Rousseaux, André, ' Un fidèle et un saint'. *Revue Universelle*, Sept. 15, 1934.
Ryan, Mary, *Introduction to Paul Claudel*. Cork Univ. Press, 1951.
Samareille, Jean, *L'Octave de la création ou la catholicité du monde selon Paul Claudel*. *Témoignages*, La Pierre qui vire, Book II, pp. 3–21.
Samson, Rev. P., *La Musique du vers claudélien*.
Sells, H. L. and Gridlestone, C. M., Introduction to their edition of *L'Annonce faite à Marie*.
Sherer, Jacques, *La dramaturgie classique en France*. Nizet, Paris.
Targue, Léon-Paul, *A Paul Claudel*. N.R.F., Vol. I, pp. 429–431.
Thibaudet, Albert, *Positions et propositions, Ecoute, ma fille*. August 1, 1934.
Truc, Gonzague, *Paul Claudel*. N.R.C.
Ursula, Sister Saint, ' Symbolism in Claudel's *Tête d'or*'. *The Commonweal*, Oct. 12, 1927.
Varillon, François, *La vocation de Paul Claudel*. *Cité Nouvelle*, Lyon, Jan. 15, 1943. Cf. Paul Claudel, *Etudes*, May 5 and 20, 1935.
Willems, Dom Walter, *Introduction au Soulier de Satin*. Bruxelles, édit. Universelle, 1939.

OTHER USEFUL BOOKS

Archer, William, *The Old Drama and the New*. Heinemann, 1923.
Cocteau and Maritain, *Art and Faith*.
Copeau, J., *Critique d'un autre temps*.
Duke, Ashley, *Modern Dramatists*. The University Library.
— *The Scene is Changed*. Macmillan.
Marriott, J. W., *The Theatre*. Harrap.
— *Modern Drama*. Nelson.
Stanislavski, *The Art of the Stage*. Faber and Faber.